YOU CAN DO THE IMPOSSIBLE

FIVE SECRETS TO MAKING IT HAPPEN

by

N. George Utuk, Ph.D.

Copyright © 2005 by N. George Utuk, Ph.D.

You Can Do The Impossible
by N. George Utuk, Ph.D.

Printed in the United States of America

ISBN 1-59781-574-8

All rights reserved solely by the author. The author guarantees all contents are original and do not infringe upon the legal rights of any other person or work. No part of this book may be reproduced in any form without the permission of the author. The views expressed in this book are not necessarily those of the publisher.

Unless otherwise indicted, all Scriptures quotations are taken from the King James Version of the Bible.

Scriptures quotations marked (NIV) are taken from the Holy Bible: New International Version®. NIV®. Copyright © 1973, 1978, 1984 by International Bible Society.

Scriptures quotations marked (NKJV) are taken from The New King James Version. Copyright © 1982 by Thomas Nelson, Inc.

Verses marked TLB are taken from The Living Bible, copyright © 1971. Used by permission of Tyndale House Publishers, Inc., Wheaton, Illinois 60189. All rights reserved.

Scriptures quotations marked (NLT) are taken from The New Living Translation. Copyright © 1996 by Tyndale House Publishers, Inc.

www.xulonpress.com

Introduction

You can do the impossible. You can walk on water. As a matter of fact, you were made for the impossible because God your Father is the God of the impossible.

The only thing standing between you and your achievement of the seemingly impossible is your comfortable position. If you watch very carefully you will see Jesus coming to you on the water. If you listen attentively, you will recognize His voice speaking to calm your fears. If you ask Him, He will invite you to come and walk on the water with Him.

Walking on water usually involves attempting to do something you have never done before. For the believer in Christ this always involves a **faith-walk.** For most people, at the initial stage this is usually quite scary and uncomfortable. However, with practice, what was scary at first becomes a normal lifestyle. The initial fears usually disappear with practice.

For some walking on water may involve going back to finish school or some other project they left unfinished. For others it may involve leaving a comfortable job position to start their own business. For some pastors it may involve taking steps of faith to start a building program. For many others walking on water may involve leaving a secular job position to enter full-time Christian ministry. Your walk on the water may not be the same as mine. Find out what yours is, step out of your comfortable boat, and do it.

What is your answer to God's invitation to take an adventure in faith with Him? Will you respond promptly and positively to this invitation? Or will you hesitate and thus miss an opportunity to experience the unusual and to grow?

It is clear from God's Word that if you have faith as a grain of a mustard seed you can say to the mountain, "Move!" and it will obey you *(Matt. 17: 20)*. To me this means that if you have a simple living faith that is planted in the extraordinary God, you can do the impossible.

Quite often believers ask the same question that the disciples asked Jesus! "Why can't we do the things you seem to do so easily?" Jesus' answer to them was, "You didn't have enough faith" *(Matt. 17:20 NLT)*. The answer to this question today is not different from the one Jesus gave the disciples a little over two thousand years ago. One thing we must realize is that if we desire to do what Jesus did, then we must be willing to act the way He did.

Having enough faith has to do more with having a living faith than with just having more faith. What we need to enable us to do the impossible is the kind of faith that holds on to what we believe even when doing so makes us look ridiculous and weird to the natural person. It is the kind of faith, as someone has put it, "that doesn't need other people's approval and doesn't care whether or not you fit in." This is the faith that enabled Jesus to heal the sick, raise the dead and walk on water. It is this kind of faith that enabled Peter to walk on water and heal the crippled man at the entrance to the temple *(Acts 3:6)*.

In ***You Can Do the Impossible*** you will learn five simple secrets to doing the impossible. You will discover that those who walk on water or do uncommon things are usually ordinary people who believe in the extraordinary God. Specifically, you will discover that the five secrets to doing the impossible include:

1. **Stepping Out to walk on water**
2. **Learning to take one step at a time**
3. **Living with God's purpose in mind**
4. **Understanding the importance of God's timing**
5. **Learning to expect and to walk in divine favor**

This book is the product of many years of personal study and walk with God. That is why it is full of personal testimonies. My prayer is that by reading this book you will be motivated to step out of your comfortable boat and walk on the water with Jesus. So go ahead and enjoy the book. But even more than that, apply the principles to your personal life as you read it.

Acknowledgment

In putting this project together many people were involved to whom I am very grateful. However, due to space constraint I may not be able to mention everyone involved in making this project possible. I want every one who helped in one way or another to know that I am grateful for the help.

First I want to give thanks to **God** by whose grace I have been able to undertake and finish this project. Then I want to acknowledge my wife and ministry partner, **Enobong Utuk,** for the moral support and encouragement she gave me while I was undertaking the project of writing this book. She also read and corrected the transcripts for which I am grateful.

Ibiangake Nseobong Utuk, my daughter, **Imayak Umoh,** my nephew, **Peter Keilman,** my God-son and **Angela Miller** read, corrected the transcript and offered some useful suggestions for which I am also grateful. **Lee Lynwood** my administrative assistant was very helpful in typing some of the chapters and setting up the whole work. Enobong and I are thankful to God for bringing Lee to the ministry. She has been a very useful tool in the Lord's hands.

This acknowledgment would not be complete without the mention of my long time friend and ministry partner since high school days, **Dr. Imeh D. Ebong.** He also read the transcripts and made some suggestions that were incorporated into the final product. Brother **Enefiok Umana,** a longtime friend and a brother in the Lord read some parts of the original transcript and suggested some changes. I am grateful to them.

Finally, I want to acknowledge and thank all the members of the **Abundant Life Word Fellowship** and the partners of **The Word of Faith Ministries, Inc.** for encouraging me to write this book.

Dedication

This book is dedicated to God's glory for His encouragement and support throughout all the years we have been in the ministry.

To my parents **George and Cecilia Utuk** who have gone home to be with the Lord. They both taught me at an early age the importance of putting God first in my life and totally depending on Him to supply all my needs.

To my dear wife and ministry partner **Enobong Utuk,** who has stood with me through good and very trying times in the ministry. She is a great woman of God and a wonderful motivator to me.

To my daughter **Ibiangake Utuk** who extended to me a thousand percent support when I first decided to quit my secular job to go into full time ministry of the Word. After fifteen years in ministry she still remains one of my strongest supporters.

To my brother Elder Edet George Utuk who has been my spiritual model and mentor for years I dedicate this book.

To all our **friends** and **partners** all over the world who have contributed financially to make it possible for us to remain a viable ministry.

The Abundant Life Word Fellowship members have enthusiastically supported this ministry for years. Enobong and I love you and always thank God for you.

Finally, I dedicate this book to all the partners of **The Word of Faith Ministries, Inc.** who strongly suggested that I write a book to share our experience with the Lord during the years. This is your book. Enobong and I pray that it blesses you.

CONTENTS

Part 1: Stepping out to walk On Water 15
Chapter 1   Step out of your comfortable position 17
Chapter 2   Be ready for some challenges 25
Chapter 3   Recognize reasons for challenges 35
Chapter 4   It does not require extraordinary faith 43

Part 2: One Step at a Time 61
Chapter 5   Daily trust is essential 63
Chapter 6   You must yield the control 73
Chapter 7   Fear: Your greatest enemy 79

Part 3: Living with God's Purpose 89
Chapter 8   Discover your purpose 91
Chapter 9   Establish a Strong Spiritual Base 99
Chapter 10   Develop your life vision 105
Chapter 11   Purpose: The most important
             driving force 113
Chapter 12   Develop a high and balanced
             self-esteem 119
Chapter 13   Time: The Most Important Gift
             from God 129

Part 4: In Its Time..135
Chapter 14   Timing: a very important element 137
Chapter 15   Two calls: to love and then to serve.............147
Chapter 16   He will never Fail 153

Part 5: Walking In Divine Favor 159
Chapter 17   The neglected spiritual tool 161
Chapter 18   Your year of divine favor............................169

We Would Like To Hear From You............................177

YOU CAN DO THE IMPOSSIBLE:

YOU CAN WALK ON THE WATER

PART ONE

STEPPING OUT TO WALK ON WATER

CHAPTER ONE

STEPPING OUT TO WALK ON WATER:
STEP OUT OF YOUR COMFORTABLE POSITION

―⇌⇋―

Then Peter called him, "Lord, if it is really you, tell me to come to you by walking on the water." "All right, come," Jesus said. So Peter went over the side of the boat and walked on the water towards Jesus (Matt. 14:28-39 NLT).

Anyone can do the impossible. Anyone can do the extraordinary because we were made for the impossible and the extraordinary. No one is an exception. However, there are some conditions necessary for doing the extraordinary and the impossible. One of those is the willingness to step out of your comfortable position and undertake a *faith-walk* with Jesus.

A FAITH-WALK IS A JOURNEY WITH GOD

The word *"walk"* has become more popular today in the United States than it has ever been. Many people wake up in the morning to take a *"walk"* before going to work. Others can't wait to get home after work to get in their *"walk"*. Even dogs are subjected to "walking" as a form of exercise. Yes, in these days of the resurgence in the relationship between regular exercise and good health, the word *"walk"* has become a household word.

At first glance it may seem like the word has just suddenly become popular. However, a careful examination of the Scriptures shows that there is nothing new about the importance of this word.

Throughout the Scriptures are records of very important "walks". The book of Genesis, for example, records the story of God's walk in the Garden of Eden after man's fall from His grace *(Gen. 3:8)*. Also in *Gen. 5:24* we read, *"Enoch walked with God; and he was not, for God took him."* In *Genesis 22:1-19* is the story of Abraham's famous *walk* to Mount Moriah to sacrifice his only son Isaac at God's command. In *Joshua 6*, is the record of Israel's walk around the city of Jericho that brought about this city's destruction. In *2 Kings 2* we read of the famous *walk* of Elijah and his servant Elisha from the city of Gilgal to the river Jordan where Elijah was taken to Heaven.

In the New Testament there are also records of some very significant walks. Some examples include 1) the disciple's *walk* with Jesus towards the city of Emmaus, 2) Saul's *walk* towards Damascus to persecute Christians, 3) Jesus' *walk* from Pilate's palace to Golgotha, where He was crucified and, of course, 4) the acclaimed *walk* of Peter on the water recorded in *(Matt. 27:22-32)*. To the serious students of the Bible, these walks are of very important spiritual significance.

Indeed, the term **walk** is a very important one in the Christian faith. It is the term used throughout the Scripture to describe a person's conduct and lifestyle in relationship to God. For instance God reminded Eli, the Old Testament prophet, of how He promised that he and his family would *"walk before (Him) forever"* *(1 Sam. 2:30)*. David the psalmist warns us not to *"walk in the counsel of the ungodly"* *(Psalm 1:1)*.

In the New Testament the Apostle Paul instructs us to *"walk in newness of life" (Rom. 6:4)*, *"not walking as mere men" (ICor. 3:3)* or *"walking in craftiness" (2Cor. 4:2)* but to *"walk in the manner worthy of the calling"* with which we had been called *(Eph. 4:1)*. For the true Christian, this process is usually referred to as *A Walk of Faith*. In this study, we shall examine some principles involved in this journey with God.

PETER'S WALK ON THE WATER

This story, of all the *walks* mentioned, has become the most famous one. This is not because of the walk in itself, but because of its spiritual significance. Peter's walk on the water symbolizes an act of obedience in simple faith. It illustrates what happens when an ordinary man is willing to step out in faith on God's invitation.

This story demonstrates the result of any obedient response to God's invitation to walk where He walks. It is an example of what can happen when a person answers God's invitation to step out of his comfortable position to an unusual experience. In this story we capture the picture of what happens when a man is willing to step out of the usual to attempt, by God's grace, what he could not do in his natural strength.

We find examples of such invitations throughout the Scripture. One Old Testament example, among many, is the story of Israel crossing the river Jordan on their push into the Promised Land. At a point during this exercise, the river Jordan presented a huge obstacle to the Israelites. They came to the Jordan during the flood season, which made the river impassable. However, God commanded them to get ready to cross the river. He was going to provide a way through the problem for them.

As we examine this story, we must bear in mind that most of the Israelites in this generation had never seen anything like this. Most of them were not born when God parted the Red Sea for their parents and grandparents as they were coming out of Egypt. They probably heard the account of the story but they had never experienced anything like it.

God had enough power to make the water disappear

before them but He did not. He could have caused a bridge to appear across the water but He did not. Instead, he commanded the priests to carry the Ark and stand in the river. They were told that *"as soon as the priests who carried the ark of the LORD - the Lord of all the earth - set foot in the Jordan, its waters flowing downstream will be cut off and stand up in a heap"(Josh. 3:13)*. As soon as the priests did what God instructed them to do, He followed through with a corresponding action by fulfilling His promise to stop the river.

THE SAME, YESTERDAY, TODAY AND FOREVER

Do you know that God still extends such invitations to ordinary believers who are willing to accept them? Yes, He still does. Now let me ask you a question, my friend: Is God, right now, challenging you to step out of your comfortable position in life to try something you have never done before? If so, what is your response to this challenge?

Let me suggest that you do not hesitate to obey whenever God invites you to try something you have never done. When He extends an invitation to you to try something different, just step out in faith and obedience. As you do so, expect Him to use the situation to demonstrate His awesome power on your behalf. Don't ever deny Him the opportunity to use you and to be God in your life.

I can hear someone asking, "But what if I run into some problems trying to answer His call?" Do not panic should you ever run into any challenges in the course of obedience to God. Instead, stand on the promises in His Word while expecting His intervention on your behalf. In the meantime, seek godly counsel and leadership. As you receive godly counsel, be ready to follow the instructions and expect God to come through for you in honor of your obedience.

Always bear in mind that nothing much will ever change in your life until you are willing to step out of your comfortable position. Your life position will remain the same until you are ready to try something you have not done before. In other words, nothing will change in your life unless you are willing to step out in faith. There is a new world out there full of adventure, waiting for those who are willing to venture out in defiance to their doubts and fears.

There is a new world out there waiting to be explored by those who are willing to step out in answer to God's call. It is reserved for those who are not afraid to venture out into the unknown. This is a land that is reserved for only the bold and daring. The fearful and cowards will never have a taste of it. Will you go with me for an adventure into this beautiful and exciting country? I pray that you do.

A RELIABLE SCRIPTURAL MODEL

A close study of the Scripture reveals a consistent series of events that take place when God calls people to venture out into the unknown. The first thing that usually happens in this process is God extending *His call* to an individual. This was the case with the Old Testament believers such as Abraham, Moses, Joshua, Gideon, Esther, Jonah and Jeremiah. In the New Testament we see the same pattern with Peter, Paul and the rest of the other disciples.

Such an invitation may not always require doing something extraordinary. However, it always involves a challenge to venture out into an unfamiliar territory. The invitation, when first received, usually evokes *fear* and *trembling* on the part of the person invited. This is because the call generally involves the undertaking of tasks that are frightening to most people at the initial stage.

The fear in many cases derives from a sense of inadequacy as was the case with Moses (*Exodus 3: 7-11*). Sometimes it may be the fear of failure. This usually involves a reluctance to answer the call for fear that one might not complete the assignment successfully. Many times the fear is that of what people might say or do to us if we answer the invitation. A typical example is the story of the Israelites in *Numbers 13.*

Some people are reluctant to answer God's call because they are afraid of His punishment. They are scared that if they fail to accomplish the task successfully God might punish them. This was the case with the man who was entrusted with one talent for investment *(Matthew 25: 24-25).*

Sometimes the fears derive from the concern that a positive response to God's invitation might interfere with one's private wishes and personal interest. This was the case with the prophet Jonah *(Jonah 1: 1-3, 3: 1-4).* In this particular situation, Jonah's desire to see the Ninevites punished came in direct conflict with God's desire to forgive and save them. Consequently, Jonah rejected God's invitation to cooperate with Him. Instead of traveling five hundred miles to answer God's invitation, he decided to travel two thousand miles to escape from God's presence. This is the typical reaction of those who try to run away from God's invitation. Such people are usually willing to pay any price to remain in disobedience to God's call.

The initial fear and trembling is more often than not accompanied by **REASSURANCE** from God of His presence and support. In the case of Moses, God assured him that he would be given what to say *(Ex. 3: 11-14).* In Gideon's situation the Angel of God informed him that he had been equipped for the task. He was also assured that God's presence was going with him *(Judges 6:7-16).* In essence, God was reminding Gideon that with His presence and support he did not have to be afraid. With God on his side Gideon had all he needed to get the job done. It's amazing how God always sees the potential in us that we very often fail to recognize. How reassuring it is to know that He will always provide for us the necessary resources for His assignments!

God's promise to be with us and to supply all our needs

is meant to move us to the place of **TRUST** in Him. Nevertheless, just trusting in God will not do any good unless we translate that trust into a **DECISION** to obey. Like Abraham, Moses and Gideon, some people will cash in that trust for obedience. However, as in the case of the eight spies in *Numbers 13:16-33*, the rich young ruler in *Mark 10:17-31* and the prophet Jonah some will reject the call. Nevertheless, the call always presents one with the opportunity to make a decision.

A positive response to God's invitation always leads to the triumph over doubt, fear and indecision. It always imparts in the one involved more grace to answer the next call from God. Some of us reading the story of Abraham in *Gen. 22:1-19* may wonder how he could bear to offer up his son Isaac for sacrifice. What we tend to forget is that this was not the first time he was instructed to give up his son. He already had a similar experience when he was instructed to send away Ishmael *(Gen. 21: 8-14)*. If you would learn to obey God when He invites you to walk by faith in the so-called little situations, you would pave the way to being obedient the next time He extends an invitation to you.

THE INEVITABLE CHANGE

God's invitation will inevitably produce *a change* in those invited. Those who give a positive response to God's call inevitably end up learning how to grow spiritually, even through their shortcomings. Those who reject the call also get changed. They frequently become resentful towards God, jealous and bitter towards those who accept God's call. They also tend to be more resistant to their next call than they were to the first.

Today, God still extends His invitation to us in the different aspects of our lives. The answer to His call always sets in motion consequences far beyond any human comprehension. The response to God's invitation will set in motion dynamics that will change your life for time and eternity.

So let me ask you again, dear friend, what is your answer to the particular invitation that God has extended to you? Will you accept this invitation or not? Your answer to this critical question will make a great impact, not only on your own life but that of others. I pray that the Lord will enable you give a positive response to His invitation.

Later on in this book I will share with you a personal testimony. It is the story of how God invited me and later on both my wife and I to step out of our comfort zones and walk with Him into the unknown. That unknown for me involved leaving my family and friends in 1973 to go to South Wales where I attended the Bible College to prepare for the ministry to which God was calling me. Later on, in 1990, He invited both of us to found The Word of Faith Ministries, Inc.

We went through all the steps I have described as we accepted the invitation and stepped out of our comfort zone to walk where He walked. Today, after fifteen years, we are still walking on the water with Him. Of course, there have been times when we felt that we were going to sink. But He has never allowed this to happen. Instead, He always reached out to hold us when we called for help.

Today, to His glory, we have become a symbol of what God can do through those who have very little natural resources but a lot of trust in Him. Through us He has demonstrated that if you can just follow Him in simple faith He will watch over you and provide for you every step of the way.

If God has invited you to step out of your comfortable position to walk on water with Him, I want to encourage you to obey him. If you do, you will have the greatest adventure of your life. The road to obedience may not always be an easy one but believe me, it will be the most exciting road you have ever walked.

CHAPTER TWO

STEPPING OUT TO WALK ON THE WATER: *BE READY FOR SOME REAL CHALLENGES*

So Peter went over the side of the boat and walked on the water towards Jesus. But when he looked around at the high waves, he was terrified and began to sink. "Save me Lord," he shouted (Matthew 14:28-30).

BE READY FOR REAL CHALLENGES

In our last study we discovered how God would invite ordinary people to attempt naturally impossible tasks. Those who accept the invitation get blessed. The others become bitter and sometimes more resistant to God's next invitation. But what is it that enables some to answer God's call and others to reject the same call? The answer is **_FAITH_**.

FAITH IS ASSURANCE OF A DESIRED END

The Bible defines faith as the assurance of things hoped for and the evidence of things not seen (Heb. 11:1). The two most important terms in this biblical definition of faith are ***assurance*** and ***evidence.*** In other words, genuine faith in God first involves an assurance that whatever God has promised me is mine even though it may not seem possible in the natural to obtain it. For example, the Bible tells us that "(Abraham) was absolutely convinced that God was able to do anything He promised" (Rom. 4:21NLT) "even though such promise seemed utterly impossible" (Rom. 4:18 NLT).

Secondly, faith in God's promise is the evidence that I can present as proof that what God has promised is mine, although I have not yet seen it in the natural. Someone has defined faith as "that which enables us to step on the invisible bridge waiting to support us while we seek to cross the seemingly bottomless pit between our present status and our God-ordained destiny."

In this sense, we can say that faith can transform the so-called impossibility into possibility. Faith enables ordinary people to attain what is humanly impossible and cross chasms that are naturally un-crossable. No foe can defeat anybody with the right kind of faith. There is no obstacle that can stop any man with the God–kind of faith (Mark 11: 22-24).

It may surprise some of you to know that even the non-Christians, to some extent, operate by natural faith. This is true because without a certain measure of faith no one could get into his car in the morning to go to work, no pilot could get into the cockpit to fly a plane and no astronaut would be able to get into the spaceship to take off into space.

Without faith we would still be riding horses instead of driving automobiles. Without faith we would still be using candles instead of the electric light. All Christians would be living in bondage to various sins and vices without faith. It is faith that enables us to trust our whole life and future to the God we do not see. As one person has put it, *"Faith combines with action in an incredible explosion of power."*

Everyone to some extent lives by faith. The big difference is in where you put your faith and trust. Some put their faith in the car, spaceship, aircraft, or even their natural abilities, which may function today and break down tomorrow. The good news is that faith in the living God will never fail, because God does not change. So if there is anything worth investing your faith in, it is the living God who created you.

NO EXCEPTION TO THE RULES

Let me say that walking by faith in God will not exempt anyone from the trials and challenges of life. As a matter of fact, there would be no need to walk by faith in God if there were no challenges in life. Anyone seeking to walk by faith will run into challenges and oppositions. Those challenges, however, will call for the exercise of more faith. Those attempting to take steps of faith will most likely run into one or more of the following:

1) ***Unexpected Problems***: The story of the disciples in *Matt. 14:22-33* demonstrates the unexpected problems that arise while we are walking in obedience. While trying to cross the Sea of Galilee in obedience to their Master the disciples ran into an unexpected storm, which posed an enormous threat to them.

Another example is the story of Joseph following the famous God-given dream that he would become a prominent leader *(Gen. 37:5-11)*. On his way to realizing the fulfillment of this dream Joseph was forced to unexpectedly stop at the pit, at Potiphar's house, and in prison before getting to his final destination, which was Pharaoh's palace. It is doubtful that Joseph dreamt about being dumped in the pit, sold to slavery, wrongly accused and put in prison before finally becoming a leader. Unfortunately this is the path that led to the destiny that God had for him.

Similarly, after he was anointed to be the king of Israel David encountered all kinds of unexpected problems while waiting to ascend the throne. However, one thing that you must note about all these Bible characters is that they never allowed any unexpected problems to stop them from continued belief in God and their pursuit of their assignments. Furthermore, nothing that they experienced caused them to become bitter or vengeful towards those that Satan used against them.

There are lessons that we can learn from these truly

successful Bible characters. First and most importantly, you must never let unexpected problems stop you from pursuing your dreams. Instead, be determined that you will face and overcome them through your faith in God and through perseverance. This is what the *faith-walk* is all about. Secondly, you must never allow your circumstances to dictate the way you relate to those who hurt you or others for that matter. Instead, always make sure that you relate to people according to God's Word. In this way you can be assured of God's presence, protection, and provision all the way in your journey towards your destiny.

2) **_Unanticipated Delays_**: The fact that you are walking by faith in God does not guarantee that doors will be open when you desire to walk through them. It does not mean that things will always run as fast and as smooth as you would expect them to. It does not mean that you will never experience setbacks or delays. As Dr. Leroy Thompson, Sr. has well said, *"God sometimes permits a block and a timeout in our lives in order to set up for us a touchdown."*

Yes, you will sometimes experience unexpected delays in your life. In the natural no one wants these delays and setbacks. Nevertheless, these permitted delays are usually necessary to enable God to set up for us some crucial appointments. Furthermore, the delay periods are often used by God to prepare us for future assignments.

The stories of Joseph and David are two typical examples that illustrate the above point. They both were called to be prominent leaders when they were young. In both cases, God permitted delays to these positions while using the period of delay to develop the character and leadership qualities in these young men.

One lesson to learn here is not to be frustrated if God seems to delay the fulfillment of His plan in your life. Instead, use the time to prepare yourself by getting into His Word, which will enable you to develop your character.

Furthermore, use this time to learn the skills that will be needed when you are promoted to the next level. You don't want to be promoted to the next level without the necessary skills to enable you to function on that level. You also don't want to be promoted to the next level without mastering this present level.

As believers in God it is important to always bear in mind that the purpose of our faith is *not* to change God's will for our lives. Rather, our faith must become God's agent in fulfilling His plan for us. For instance, if God's plan is that you go through some situations to prepare you for your final position in life, as in the case of Joseph and David, your faith in God should sustain you through the process. In such situations your faith in God ought to be the security guard that protects God's purpose in your life until it is fulfilled.

Like Shadrach, Meshach and Abednego you will discover through God's dealing with you that His presence with you will provide a shield to protect you from being destroyed by the enemy's fire. The fire, instead of destroying you, will refine you and reposition you for greater blessing and usefulness.

Furthermore, you will discover that circumstances that cause others to surrender, fall, or quit will give you an opportunity to learn how to triumph even in the most trying situations. After it all, you will be qualified to minister to every person that God will send into your life, who may be going through situations like yours.

Finally, if you allow God to utilize these circumstances to shape you, then at the end "you will be ready for anything, strong in character, full and complete" *(Jam. 1:4 TLB).* Nonetheless, if you resent and rebel against God's dealing with you, don't be surprised if, as it was with the children of Israel, it takes you forty years to complete an eleven-day journey *(Deut. 1:1-8).*

3) ***Unusual pressure***: Everyone seeking to fulfill God's purpose for his life, at some point, will come under unusual pressure. This is generally the case when we encounter unexpected problems or unusual delays and challenges. During such times, there is always the temptation to act in such a way as to get out from under the pressure.

A typical example was when God delayed the fulfillment of the promise to give a child to Abraham. Instead of waiting for God to fulfill that promise Abraham succumbed to the pressure by Sarah. She suggested to Abraham to speed up the fulfillment of the promise by having a child by Hagar, her maid. As a result of yielding to the pressure by Sarah, Ishmael was born.

As is usually the case in such situations, at first it appeared that Ishmael had met the need for a son that Abraham had. At the end this turned out not to be the case. Initially, Ishmael and Isaac, the promised child, lived together without any problem. However, it was just a matter of time before the hidden problems surfaced. The problems first started when Ishmael the child produced in the flesh began to mock Isaac, the child of God's promise. The problem became more complex when God had to make Abraham send away Ishmael so that Isaac could grow in a peaceful environment. Though reluctant at first, Abraham had to let go Ishmael in order to experience God's full blessing on his life.

Ishmael in this story represents anything that we produce without God's endorsement. It could be a job position, a relationship or any other thing. There are always some problems associated with the Ishmaels of this world: 1) Just because God allows your Ishmael to live under the same roof with your Isaac does not mean that this is God's perfect will for you. 2) Your Ishmael will, at a point, start mocking your Isaac if you don't get rid of him. 3) Ishmaels are very easy to produce but very difficult to get rid of. 4) To have God's full blessing on your life you will have to let go whatever your Ishmael may be.

The final lesson to learn from the story is that you must not make crucial decisions based on the need to relief pressure. Such actions usually help Satan fulfill his purpose, which is to pin your back against the wall so that you will abandon the God-given strategy for your assignment.

Some of you reading this book are exactly at the point of doing just that. Nevertheless, you don't have any excuse to go through with such a decision now that this timely message from God has come for your warning. You need to continue to wait on God until He reveals His perfect will to you.

If Satan can get you to abandon your God-given game plan, he will defeat you very easily. So, when you feel like you are under pressure, you need to pull back and regroup. Spend this time praying for His grace and wisdom. This will help you recapture the momentum so that you can continue to steer in the right course.

Coaches and sport managers use this strategy all the time. Whenever a basketball coach, for example, feels that his team is under too much pressure from the opposing team, he will call for a time out to enable them to regroup. Often, a good coach will use this time to reorganize and consult with his assistants. Then he will return his players to the court after they have regrouped and refocused.

Undoubtedly, maintaining the right course may result in a temporary slowing down of your progress. Yet always remember that if you compromise your important values to gain something, you will eventually lose the gains you made.

It's not worth having it, if you are going to disobey God in the process to obtain it. The truth is that there is time for everything *(Eccl. 3:1-3)*. Everyone has his due season *(Heb. 6:12)*. Every truly successful person in this world paid his dues to get to where he is now. Nothing comes without a price tag and no success comes overnight. So don't be too much in a hurry. Take your time and be patient and God will reward both your diligence and patience.

Moses is another example of one who succumbed to pressure and consequently lost his blessing. When Moses was pressured to give water in the wilderness to the Israelites, he got agitated and as a result lost his focus. Under that pressure he struck the rock instead of speaking to it as God instructed him *(Num. 20:2-11)*. As a result of that disobedience he lost the privilege of leading the Israelites into the Promised Land *(Num. 20:12)*. Don't ever allow unusual pressure to push you out of God's designed course – it's not worth losing your blessing.

FACING UNEXPECTED SITUATIONS

There are four very important steps you must take when you run into unusual and tough situations during your faith-walk:

1) *Pray* – Whenever you walk into unexpected situations in your life you must pull back and pray. Prayer is a means of communication with God. God's instruction to us in His word is to **be anxious for nothing but in everything by prayer, petition and thanksgiving to make our request known to Him** *(Phil 4:6-8)*. This is why we must talk to God before talking to anyone else about our problems. This is the reason that we must pray instead of grumbling and complaining about our situations.

Sometimes when you pray, God will drop the needed answer directly into your spirit. At other times, He will direct you to the person who will have the answer you need to resolve your problem. Whatever the case, you must make a determined effort to pray, even when you feel like complaining – which only helps to raise the level of your stress and anxiety.

Prayer will help to calm and still your emotions. This consequently will enable you to think right and make informed and proper decisions. So, whenever you feel stressed out, stop everything and pray. Most of our problems would be properly resolved if we would stop, pray and wait on God for answers.

2) ***Think and Talk*** - Whenever possible, seek mature counseling before making your final decision. Some problems can be resolved by careful thought and rearranging your priorities. However, discussion and proper godly counsel can also help resolve some of the most annoying issues in your life. Therefore, if you are still confused after prayer and careful thought, then you need to consult with your spiritual counsel. The word of God tells us that plans go wrong with too few counselors; (but) many counselors bring success *(Prov. 15:22 TLB)*.

3) <u>***Listen Quietly To God***</u> – God wants to give us the right answers in every stressful situation we face *(Is. 30:12)*. The problem is that most people become so preoccupied with trying to find the answer that they neither think, pray, nor listen *(Is. 30:1-5)*. However, you must think, pray, and listen when confused instead of getting bogged down with trying to resolve the problem.

Some people complain that God does not speak when they need to hear from Him. As someone has well put it, *"God is not mute"*. If it is true that He is not mute, then someone must not be listening if they haven't heard Him. I cannot over-emphasize the need to be still and listen carefully to God when answers are needed in situations you are facing. You must learn to sit still and listen to God before proceeding in any direction. Doing so will save you from many hours of wondering what could have been if you had listened to Him.

4) <u>***Obey Promptly***</u> – Prompt obedience when God speaks is a major aspect of the faith-walk. If you are not ready to act on the instructions God will give you, you might as well forget about resolving your problem. God is quite clear in His word when He says that obedience is better than sacrifice *(I Sam. 15:22)*. The least we can do for Him when He instructs us is to obey and promptly at that.

Some people would rather ignore God's instructions when they are under the heat. The same people will expect Him to help them clean up their mess when they begin to reap the harvest of their disobedience.

Listen to me, dear friend: though obedience to God may sometimes seem to be the hardest thing to do, nevertheless, it's always the best thing for you. The price of disobedience is always far greater than any price you may have to pay for obedience to God.

Let me repeat that the walk of faith does not exclude challenges. As a matter of fact, it is the challenges that make the walk one of faith. When you are challenged during your faith-walk, remember to talk to the Lord (i.e. pray), think and listen to informed and godly counsel. Finally, develop a habit of acting promptly on any word that God gives to you. Follow these steps and you can always count on God to help you get to your destination in spite of the challenges you may encounter.

CHAPTER THREE

STEPPING OUT TO WALK ON THE WATER: *YOU MUST UNDERSTAND REASONS FOR CHALLENGES*

…But when He saw the wind He was afraid, and, beginning to sink, he cried out, "Lord, save me." Immediately Jesus reached out his hand and caught Him (Matt. 14:30-31).

WHY DOES GOD ALLOW CHALLENGES?

As powerful as He is, why doesn't God stop problems before they reach His children? I believe that there are a number of reasons that God sometimes allows us to encounter problems, even though He has all the ability to stop them.

1. A TEST OF YOUR FAITH

Your faith in God and His promises will be tested in the process of seeking to walk in obedience to Him *(Matt. 14:22-24, 13:20-21)*. The question is never whether your faith will be tested but when it will be tested. The other question is whether or not you will maintain your trust in Him during the test.

Your claims to Christ will be challenged but will you abandon the call and return to the world when subjected to pressure? Or will you use your faith in God and His Word to fight back the opposing forces? These are the questions you must ask yourself. The quality and level of your faith in God will definitely be revealed during the challenge by unexpected problems, delays and unusual pressures.

This is one reason why James, in his letter, instructed believers to *rejoice* when their faith is tested. By no means did James advocate the denial of the pains involved during the testing of your faith. Rather, he was saying that you should rejoice because the tests will reveal your ability to utilize God's word to confront and resolve problems in your life *(Jam. 1:2)*.

Your level of maturity in Christ and your ability to maintain your convictions will also be revealed during the trying and testing times in your life *(Jam. 1:3)*. So don't panic when your faith is tested. Instead, make a quality decision not to cast away your confidence in God and His promises no matter how intense the trial may be *(Heb. 10:35-39)*.

Be patient and keep working His Word while you answer His invitation to walk where He walks. Just as He did with Peter, He will come to your aid if you ever have a reason to ask for it *(Matt. 14:25)*.

The worst thing you can do when you are tested is to panic or to doubt what God told you at the beginning of your call. Doubt or panic will cause you to lose focus and begin to sink *(Matt. 14:31)*. For that reason, whenever you run into tight spots during your walk with God, always remember how He intervened for you in other situations in the past. Remind yourself that just as He came through for you in the past, He will do it again. Just be sure that you don't give up before His help arrives *(1 Pet. 4: 12-13)*.

2. A CHANGE OF DIRECTION

There are times when difficulties may indicate God's intention to change your course. That was the case with Elijah in *1 Kings 17:1-10*. At God's command Elijah went to the brook at Cherith where God provided for him as He promised. But after a while the brook from which he drank began to dry up. God then commanded him to move to another location. In this particular incident the gradual drying of the brook was an indication that God was about to change Elijah's assignment. It was not the trial of his faith.

No matter how much faith Elijah would have exercised at this point, he would not have been able to revive the brook. This is because God's presence and power had already left Cherith to the next location of Elijah's assignment - Zarepheth. God's power and presence can only be expected to manifest where His will is. Outside His will you will be operating without His power and presence.

A good example in the New Testament is when Jesus commanded the disciples to go and preach repentance, beginning in Jerusalem *(Luke 24:47)*. They were to remain in Jerusalem until they received the Holy Spirit, after which they were to take the good news to the whole world. Unfortunately, instead of obeying the Master's instruction, "they returned to Jerusalem with great joy and stayed at the temple continually praising God" *(Luke 24:52-53)*.

The result of remaining in that comfort zone instead of going out in obedience is recorded by Luke in this statement: *"On that day, a great persecution broke out against the church at Jerusalem, and all except the Apostles were scattered throughout Judea and Samaria. Godly men buried Stephen and mourned deeply for him. But Saul began to destroy the church. Going from house to house, he dragged men and women off and put them in prison"* *(Acts 8:2-3)*.

Now let's face it. There is nothing wrong with waiting on God for directions and the power to carry them out. However, there is everything wrong with refusing to move forward because we are trying to relive some experience with God we might have had in the past.

When God has an assignment for you He will do whatever it takes to get you there. If it means causing the brook to dry up on you or permitting some persecution to take place, He will do it. This is because, as the Scriptures say, all discipline may now seem to be painful rather than pleasant. Nevertheless, it will later yield a peaceful fruit of righteousness to them who have been trained by it *(Heb. 12:11)*.

God will allow situations to set in and uproot you if He knows that you will miss His call for your life by sitting around in your comfort zone. My prayer and hope is that your present problems are not caused by you trying to hold on to a position from which God has already released you.

A number of years ago, I had an experience in which the Lord had to uproot me from my comfort zone before He could promote me. That comfort zone was the job I had in a particular city before moving to Middle Georgia where we are now located. I was hired to that position at the time in my life when I really needed it. When I had it, everything went for me. The salary was good and the people were very good to me. In fact, this was the best job that I had ever had since I came to United States. After a number of years, I became so comfortable in the position that I began to see myself working it until retirement. But God had a different plan for me.

About three years after I got the job I began to experience some problems with my immediate boss who, before then, I thought was my best friend. Before I knew it, my boss hired people into two of the positions I held in the organization. Consequently, I was forced to resign and leave in near humiliation.

At the time I was angry and wondered why the Lord would have allowed that to happen to me. After all, I had served my boss and the organization faithfully and had taken that job when they really needed me. To put it mildly, I resorted to self-pity instead of seeking God's face for direction. Yet I praise the Lord who provided another position in another city with more pay before I resigned. I have since come to believe that, though God did not engineer the situations at that job place, He nevertheless, used them to move me from the position I had come to love and thus become too comfortable in.

On August 29, 1989 Enobong and I went to inform our pastor of our intention to move to another job position. We wanted him to pray for us and send us on our way. While waiting in his lounge to see him, a xerox copy of the daily devotional on his center table caught my attention. As soon as my eyes fell on the text of that day's devotion the Scriptures changed from the written word to God speaking directly to me. The devotion was from Oswald Chamber's book, ***My Utmost for His Highest*** and the text was from *John 11:40,* which says, *"...Did I not say to you that if you believe you would see the glory of God?"*

When I read that it hit me like a ton of bricks and that was God's confirmation to me that He would take care of my family if we would trust Him. With this promise from God I left to start my new job. However, a year after taking that new job the Lord spoke to Enobong and I to resign that second position and step out in faith to found The Word of Faith Ministries, Inc.

Today, to the glory of God, we both thank God for the incidents that led to my resignation from that position that brought us to this area. At the time of the incident it was almost impossible to see God's hand in it. Yet in retrospect we have come to believe that although He did not initiate the circumstances, He was always in absolute control of every event related to them.

Whatever your situation may be; let me encourage you not to give up. Instead, trust in the Lord and as best as you know how continue to do what is right. God will ultimately vindicate your cause.

I should note here that not all the changes that we may be required to make will necessarily involve a change in direction. Some may only involve some reorganization or change in method. For example, a businessman who runs into some challenges in his business needs to take some time out to pray. He needs to seek God's face concerning the root cause of his problem. If he discovers through prayer that the problem is a challenge of his faith, then he needs to stand on God's word until he receives a breakthrough *(Eph. 6:13-15)*.

On the other hand, after prayer he may discover that God is leading him towards a change in direction. Such change may not necessarily be to a new location, line of business or product. It may only involve the reorganization of the business' operational methods to enable it to produce at its maximum level. We must be so sensitive to God's voice that we are ready to move in any direction He leads, no matter how comfortable we may feel in our present position.

We must always remember that God sees and knows what we may not necessarily see or know about our future. He usually warns and prepares His children ahead of time when He foresees an impending danger. Such preparation will enable us to successfully handle the problems when they arrive. When we listen to Him and make the necessary adjustments, we always end up being blessed and therefore become a blessing to other people. Nonetheless, when we ignore or fail to recognize His warning signs, we always end up paying a high price for our ignorance or the disobedience.

Change is not usually something we want to undertake because it sometimes involves a lot of hassle. Nonetheless, we will never be able to grow unless we are willing to change. So, don't be afraid to change when necessary because sometimes it will take you to the next level of service to God *(Rom. 12:1-2)*. When God is about to move, pack your bags and be ready to move with Him. If you do, you may end up bringing a revival to the whole city as Philip did when he went to Samaria to preach as the Lord had instructed *(Acts 8: 4-8)*.

3. DISCIPLINARY ACTION

Some situations are allowed in our lives as corrective measures. In the process of serving the Lord, we at times either forget or outright ignore His instructions. In the process, we end up serving our personal interests instead of His interests.

This was the case with the prophet Jonah. God instructed the prophet to go and preach repentance to the people that he wanted God to punish. Instead of obeying God's instruction, Jonah tried to escape from His presence. In the process he ran into a storm that almost took His life and that of others. This was an example of God allowing His child to run into a difficult situation to stop him from continuing in his act of disobedience. He addressed the problem so that it would not come back in the future to haunt them. God still employs the same method whenever necessary.

Another example of God withdrawing His presence as disciplinary measure was the incident with the Israelites in *Joshua 7*. In this story, God specifically instructed the Israelites before the Jericho battle not to keep any of the things that would be abandoned by the enemy after the war. Whatever item of value was left behind was to be dedicated to the service of the Lord. Even so, in clear violation to God's instructions, a man named Achan took and hid for himself some of the war's plunder.

As a result of this blatant disobedience to God's instructions, His presence was withdrawn from Israel's army. Consequently, they suffered a defeat by a city that should not have been a challenge to them. This was God's disciplinary measure to correct His people *(Jos. 7:6-13)*. God's disciplinary actions are not meant to destroy His people *(Heb. 12:4-13)*. He would rather have them obey Him and in doing so remain under His protection *(Ps. 91:1-3)*. Yet if they deliberately defy His instructions, God will have no alternative but to allow them to have their way and later eat of its fruit.

Please note that I did not say that God sends problems to correct us. He does not. God normally corrects His children with the use of His word. Even so, He will withdraw His presence if we continuously and deliberately violate His instructions. Whenever we deliberately disobey God's instructions, we open the door to Satan taking advantage of and attacking us. In this case we can only blame ourselves, not God, for whatever happens as a result of such an open door.

God will withdraw His presence to force us to return to His Word. His presence and power are only there to protect those who live in obedience to His Word. If you ever discover that your problem is as a result of your disobedience, don't try to exercise more faith, change your location, or reorganize. Instead, repent and ask for forgiveness. Then make the required adjustments to get back to where you need to be. Then wait until He gives you further instructions before moving in any direction. Do not make a move because there is nothing else to do. God is not interested in you just being busy. The most important thing is that you live in obedience to His instructions.

BUT HOW DO WE KNOW?

How do we know what the message is when we face a particular challenge? Let me caution that you do not suddenly rush to conclusions as to what God is trying to say when you encounter trying situations in your life. This is because each situation is unique and different. Instead of rushing to easy conclusions you must **spend time seeking the Lord in prayer and the study of His Word.** Furthermore, **seek mature counsel from a pastor, minister, or a mature spiritual leader, being also ready to obey when God speaks to you.** If you are willing to follow these steps, I can guarantee that you will receive the needed direction from God. As a last word, never make any adjustments in your life without first hearing from God. ***You need Him***.

CHAPTER FOUR

STEPPING OUT TO WALK ON WATER: *IT DOES NOT REQUIRE EXTRAORDINARY FAITH*

―――◦―――

... So Peter went over the side of the boat and walked on the water towards Jesus. But when he looked around at the waves, he was terrified and began to sink. "Save me Lord!" he shouted. Instantly, Jesus reached out His hand and grabbed him" (Matt. 14:28-31).

IT DOESN'T REQUIRE EXTRAORDINARY FAITH

We learn from God's word that it is impossible to please Him without faith *(Heb. 11:6)*. In the last three chapters we examined some important aspects of the **FAITH-WALK**. Hopefully, these studies have prepared you for the promotion to the next level of your *faith-walk*. In this part of our study we shall look at some of the important qualities of the men and women who successfully engaged in this walk of faith. I pray that this study will motivate you to give a positive response to God's invitation to come and walk with Him.

1. ORDINARY PEOPLE (1Cor. 1:24-29)

Many people erroneously believe that it takes extraordinary people to walk by faith. There is nothing further from the truth. In reality, those who walk by faith are rarely extraordinary people. They are usually ordinary people who place their faith in an extraordinary God.

There was nothing extraordinary about men such as Abraham, Joseph, David, Daniel, Elijah or Elisha. Neither was there anything extraordinary about such women as Rahab, Deborah, Ruth, Esther or Mary, the mother of our Lord. All of these were ordinary human beings who believed in an extraordinary God. This is why our Lord's mother, Mary, was able to say to the angel Gabriel in the face of impossibility, ***"Behold the maiden of the Lord. Let it be to me according to your word."(Luke 1:38)***

Each of these men and women, like many of us, received God's invitation to cooperate with Him. Unlike some people who refuse to cooperate, these men and women stepped out and took advantage of the call. As a result of their willingness to cooperate with God, He rewarded them with recognition and influence. These people recognized the presence of God and stepped into it and God blessed them.

In the same way, God will accord recognition to any man or woman who is willing to step out in faith in obedience to Him *(Gen. 12:1-2)*. He will do so, especially for those willing to step out when remaining in their comfort zone would seem to be the easier option.

Maybe your step of faith will not earn you as much widespread recognition and influence as those we have just mentioned. Nevertheless, you can be sure that there are people watching you who will be greatly impacted by your decisions. So don't be afraid to step out in faith when you recognize His presence or hear His voice.

2. *ABILITY TO RECOGNIZE GOD'S PRESENCE AND HIS VOICE*

God's presence and his voice make the difference between faith, foolishness and presumption. The man of faith steps out because he senses God's presence and perceives what others do not. He steps out because he has heard from God. The foolish or presumptuous person steps out spurred on by his ego and emotions. He does so to prove that he is something, which he may not be. He is usually ignorant of God's word and despises mature godly counsel.

Peter did not just step out on the water to prove something. He did so in answer to the invitation to come and walk on the water with Jesus *(Matt. 14:29)*. In the same way, if you pay careful attention, you may see Jesus approaching you. As He approaches He may speak to you through His word or through some godly individual whose counsel you respect. If you ask for His permission, He might even invite you to come and walk on the water with Him.

Unfortunately, many of God's people fail to capture His presence when He moves. They never pay close enough attention to be able to hear Him when He speaks. Consequently, they miss opportunities to walk where He walks. These people can pass by God and not even recognize Him because He did not appear to them according to their preconceived notions. He did not drive the type of vehicle they expected of Him.

He came walking on the water instead of arriving in a ship. He dressed like a homeless drunk instead of a typical church attendee. He showed up as a prostitute instead of a virgin. He appeared as a cynical woman already divorced five times instead of a virginal, optimistic newlywed. Sometimes He shows up when we do not expect Him. If you are not expecting Jesus He may pass by without your recognition *(Mark 6:47-48)*.

Let me ask you a question, friend. Are you looking for God in every situation in which you are involved? If so, you will recognize Him when He appears. When you recognize Him, dare to ask Him to allow you the privilege of walking where He walks. Never have a preconception of how God will show up because He may surprise you.

God has an interesting sense of humor. It is always amazing to watch Him do things contrary to our natural expectations. My wife and I experience this all the time. A great example is when we prayed, believing God to send us our first ten thousand dollar donation. When He answered the prayer, He used an individual that we would have least expected to be the one carrying the answer to our prayers. The car that this man drove at the time was smoking. His clothes were not the best and certainly not name brand. I had to give him a ride to the bank in another city to withdraw the money because his car could not have made the trip. Yet this was the man that God used to answer this prayer.

The interesting thing about this whole situation was that for about three years, before the young man gave us the donation, I had tried to minister to him to no avail. For most of those three years I seemed to have gotten nowhere with him. Many times I thought about giving up but the Lord would not let me do so. So I would approach again and leave with him either a tract or one of my tapes. Meanwhile my wife and I continued to constantly intercede for the soul salvation of this young man.

During those three years I, many times, wondered whether I was walking where Jesus was or not. There was nothing in the natural that would have suggested that I was ministering to someone who would later become one of our most faithful partners in ministry. Nevertheless I continued to reach out to him in spite of the apparent rejection.

Somewhere during the process Satan began to attack this young man's mind telling him that he was going to die. As a result he grasped a Bible and locked himself in a room and begged God to save him. He told God that he was not going to leave the room unless he had the assurance that he was saved. According to him, he received that assurance when he read the Bible to *Acts 4:12* which says, *"Salvation is found in no one else, for there is no other name under heaven given to men by which we must be saved."*

After reading this scripture, he prayed in that room to receive Jesus as his personal Savior. He later told me of how a voice inside told him to come and share with me what had happened. Since that Wednesday morning when he sat on the steps of my office crying like a baby while waiting to tell me what had happened to him, we have become close friends. He has since joined our church and remains a very active member. What a wonderful God we serve!

My wife and I learned an important lesson from that situation: Never box God into your own natural way of thinking. He is much, much bigger than that. I believe that is why He declares in *Isaiah 55: 8-9, "For my thoughts are not your thoughts, neither are your ways my ways. As the heavens are higher than the earth, so are my ways higher than your ways and my thoughts higher than your thoughts."*

3. BOLDNESS AS THE LION'S (Prov. 28:1)

The initial reaction of a lion to a life-threatening situation is to retreat. However, don't you go by that initial reaction! After such initial response the lion will return, charging towards the source of threat. When he returns to face the perceived enemy, the lion will pursue and attack until the threat is either eliminated or run off. The point is this: The lion may retreat at an initial perception of threat, but a lion never flees from a threatening situation - not even from an elephant. That is why the Scriptures say that the righteous is as bold as a lion *(Prov. 28:1)*.

In general, most people (including Christians) will sense an attack of fear when they perceive an unknown and threatening situation. Satan usually attacks most believers with fear and self-doubts when they desire to do something different than they are used to. For a Christian, or any one else for that matter, to experience these feelings is not sinful, much like the temptation to sin is not a sin.

However, I also want to encourage you to never allow

fearful feelings to overpower and control you. You must resist these feelings with everything in you before they overcome and paralyze you. ***Never allow fearful feelings to dominate and eventually dictate your response to threatening situations.***

True, there are times that God will enable you to accomplish great feats without even thinking about the risks involved. During such times He, by and large, will supernaturally empty your mind of any doubts or fears. He does this so that you can flow in faith without worrying about the consequences of stepping out into the unknown.

However, these are rare occasions, in my opinion. These, I believe, are times that God just imparts on you the gift of special faith to enable you to perform special tasks. This, I believe is what happened when Elijah called down the fire on Mount Carmel *(1Kings 18)*. I also believe that this was what happened when Peter healed the crippled man at the Gate Beautiful *(Acts 3:1-10)*.

For the most part, this is not a normal lifestyle. In a normal situation, most people will sense a measure of doubt or fear when challenged to take on an unusual task. Right there, they will be faced with two choices: 1) trust and obey God or 2) succumb to fear and back off from God's call.

As we have noticed, the word of God is very clear concerning the fact that it is the wicked that flees when nothing pursues him. But the righteous are as bold as the lion *(Prov. 28:1)*. Does this necessarily mean that because one is courageous he will never feel afraid? Of course not! We all know that the absence of fear does not in any way spell the presence of courage. Indeed the absence of fear may mean that there is nothing to fear because you don't have enough courage to challenge the status quo.

While courage is not the absence of fear, nevertheless, it is courage that enables us to exercise control over fear. That was what the Psalmist meant when he cautioned us to wait on the Lord so that He will strengthen our hearts *(Psalm 34:14)*. In essence what the Psalmist meant was that if we would learn to firmly trust God in threatening circumstances, He would give us the courage needed to face such situations.

Let me emphasize again, dear friend that the threat of fear will never totally disappear as long as you continue to grow in your walk with God. Fear and growth go together, but don't give in to fear. Always remember this: Though fear will always be there, it does not have to control you. Paul, writing to young Timothy, reminded him to fan to flame of God's gift in him. He reminded Timothy that God did not give us the spirit of fear, but one of power, love, and sound mind *(2 Tim. 1: 6-7)*.

Notice what the above portion is saying. Essentially what it is saying is that though fear may be there, it does not come from God. If God is not the source of fear, where then does this attack come from? The answer is that fear is from the devil. If this is the case, then the obvious conclusion is that we must resist it with every tool that God has given to us.

I can assure you of one thing, friend. There will always be times in your life that you will have to choose between fear and the trust in God. For some of us, it may come to the point of having to choose to remain in an abusive relationship or walking out and trusting in God to protect and provide for us. For the rest of us it may involve having to choose between yielding to the fear of our peers while doing what we know to be wrong or trusting the Lord to protect us while choosing to do what we know to be right. One thing is quite certain; we will always have to choose. The question is what will you do when you come to that crossroad?

Personally, I rarely face a challenging situation in which I did not have to choose between the two options – to yield to the spirit of fear or trust and obey the Lord. But every time I chose to follow my godly convictions, I ended up with an opportunity to grow and become a better person spiritually.

Therefore, let me encourage you, dear friend, to not ever run away from fear or surrender to it. Face it and deal with it so that, if possible, you may learn something that will help in your future encounters with it. If you don't face and deal with your fears today, you will lose the opportunity to grow in your *faith-walk.* I am sure this is not what you desire for yourself.

Right now, settle once and for all that fear is an inevitable part of desiring to do anything of significance for God. Be aware of the fact that every time you venture into a new territory, Satan will loose the spirit of fear to attack you. At the same time be resolved always to confront your fears. Doing so will help you learn some things that will enable you to become a stronger and better instrument in God's hand.

Whenever the spirit of fear attacks you, confront it immediately with God's word. Declare your victory over this spirit whenever it attacks. Take authority over it in the Name of Jesus, the Anointed One. With the prophet Isaiah, proclaim in the face of fear: *"Surely God is my salvation; I will trust and not be afraid. The Lord, the Lord is my strength and my song; He has become my salvation" (Isaiah 12:2 NIV).*

Like the Psalmist you must learn to confess when Satan attacks you with fear, *"When I am afraid I will trust in you. In God whose word I praise, in God I trust; I will not be afraid. What can a mortal man do to me?" (Ps.5 6:3-4NIV).* Let me submit to you that the worst thing you can do when Satan attacks you with fear is to do nothing. At such a time, sitting around doing nothing, believing that the fear will go away, will actually cripple you. On the other hand taking a risk to confront the spirit of fear will totally rob fear of its power over you.

If you can properly deal with your fears, they will become a springboard to 1) a deeper trust in God, 2) changes that may lead to a new level of understanding of God's ways and finally 3) a new level of spiritual growth for you. Yet if you don't know how to manage your fears, they will paralyze your initiative and steal your vision. Let me emphasize again the fact that if you have never been attacked by fear, it may be an indication that you have never tried to do anything of significance for God. If this is the case, then it is no surprise that the devil has never attacked you.

The enemy employs fear as a tool to intimidate everyone, and God's people in particular. He does so in an attempt to frighten God's people out of God's designed path. However, you don't have to yield to Satan's intimidation. On the contrary, you must courageously and boldly take authority over him whenever he attacks.

Always let every attack by the enemy drive you into total dependence on God. Draw strength from His extraordinary grace for your assignment. Has He not promised in His word, *"My grace is sufficient for you, for my power is made perfect in weakness" (2 Cor.12: 8NIV)*? So whenever you feel weak and threatened, always remember that there is someone on your inside much greater and stronger than you. Submit yourself to Him, tap into His strength and resist the devil and he will have no alternative but to flee from you. *(James 4:7).*

4. WILLINGNESS TO RISK A FALL

The fourth important characteristic of those who do the impossible is the ability and willingness to risk a fall. The Book of Proverbs reminds us that, *"though the righteous man falls seven times, he rises again, but the wicked are brought down by calamity" (Prov. 24:16)*. Put it another way: Just because an Olympic sprinter, for example, trips does not necessarily mean that he has lost the race. If he regains his balance and gets back in the race, there is a possibility that he might win the race. In the same way, I want to remind you that a fall does not in any way mean that you are a failure. Actually a fall may provide you with an opportunity to learn what not to do in the next race. If you ever trip and fall in an attempt to do the impossible, get back up and start again. Falling never proves that a man is a failure but quitting or even refusing to try does.

That Peter started sinking after stepping out of the boat and walking on the water did not mean that he was a failure. The actual failures were those other disciples who could not even recognize their Master or His voice. They allowed fear to so paralyze them to the point that they failed to recognize an opportunity to experience the extraordinary.

Peter was a huge success for attempting and successfully doing what no other human being, except Jesus, had ever done. Sure, he lost his focus and as a result started to sink. Nonetheless, I imagine that he also learned the important lesson that while walking on the water you must fix your eyes, not on the storm, but on the One who called you to walk on the water with Him.

Moreover, Peter proved that if you call on Jesus even in the midst of a huge mistake, He would come to your help and even escort you to safety *(Matt. 12:29-32)*. ***Willingness to risk a fall will always provide tremendous opportunity for growth.*** And guess what! Many of the most valuable lessons we have learned in life have been from trying something that did not work – at least at the time we first tried.

HABITS ARE CULTIVATED

A very important secret to learn is that risks and comfort always grow into habits. What I mean is that the more risks you are willing to take, the more habitual taking risks will become for you. Conversely, the more you are willing to sit in comfort, over time, the more you will do so. That will become a way of thinking, a state of mind by which you live. Therefore, don't ever be afraid to take risks, especially when it is necessary to enable you to answer God's call.

Always keep in mind that the most dangerous believers to Satan are those who are not afraid to take risks for God. They are generally those who are never frightened out of God's will by problems, oppositions or critics. They possess pioneer spirits, taking risks in the process of stepping out into the unknown. They are always willing to sacrifice the present comfort for future growth. These are typically pace–setters, barrier-breakers, pioneers and symbols of courage in God's kingdom. They are the ones normally inducted into the FAITH HALL OF FAME. Those who are unwilling to take risks for God normally end up taking risks for the devil. Don't be one of those.

STEP INTO THE OUTER LIMITS

One thing about willingness to take risks is that it helps you expand your comfort zone. A comfort zone is that area within which an individual can operate without too much risk.

It is not always wrong to operate within a comfortable sphere. However, some have allowed this setting to become something they depend upon to provide safety, security and comfort apart from God. They have made this place their sanctuary when things get tough. They rely so much on it that they are unable to move when God invites them to step into the outer limits.

This zone of comfort has deprived many of the ability to make a total commitment to God. In this sense, therefore, it is wrong to remain in comfort, especially after God has extended an invitation to you to step out into an area you have never tried before.

It is normally quite frightening at the initial stage to step out of the comfort zone. However, if you patiently work long enough within the new unfamiliar territory, it will soon become a part of your comfort zone. The area that yesterday was dangerous ground, can with practice and experience become today's comfort area within to operate.

Think, for instance, about when you first started learning how to drive. For many of us it was the most frightening thing we ever attempted to do. Before, we had wondered how it was that some people could get into a car and drive with such ease. Yet we kept working on our driving skills until we could drive well enough to take a test and obtain the driver's license. Now after driving for some time we can get into the car and drive without thinking about it.

When you first started driving you never took your hands off the steering wheel for any reason. Now with years of experience you can eat, drink and talk on your cell phone all at the same time while driving. You now perform all these tasks without even being conscious of the fact that you are driving. (By the way this is not a recommended habit for any driver. It is not a good example of doing the impossible either).

Some time ago I heard someone say that everything that God calls must move. That means that if God has called you then you must be ready to move, even when such a move involves taking a risk. A further implication of this thought is that if what you are doing is of God then it should be producing. If it's not producing, then you may need to seriously seek God's face in prayer and His word to find out whether He wants you to continue doing it.

If you don't believe that you are progressing towards fulfilling your God-given purpose in your present position, then you need to pray that God will redirect your steps in the right direction. You cannot remain comfortable in the same position and expect at the same time to enjoy what God has for you down the road.

If you are praying for growth, then you must be ready to make some adjustments in your life. But let me caution that it will take a lot of courage and risk to make some of these changes.

However, you must courageously make them if you desire to experience the necessary growth and increase in your life. The more you learn to quickly make the needed changes in your life, the easier it will be to make any adjustment the next time around.

GROWTH IN THE FRUIT OF PATIENCE

In *Hebrews 6:12* Paul advised the Christians not to be lazy but to imitate those who through faith and patience inherited what was promised. Actually, the whole story of walking by faith or doing the impossible is the story of learning to grow in patience. No one should consider a faith-walk unless he or she is willing to take a course on patience.

Faith and patience are twin sisters. Abraham, Joseph, David and the disciples all had to take lessons on faith and patience. The disciples, in *Matt. 14*, had to sit in the storm for hours waiting for their Lord to come to their rescue. And even then they still had to wait until the end of the story to receive their needed breakthrough.

As human beings we have a tendency to take a snapshot of God at a particular point and use that shot to determine who He is and what He is capable of doing. But it takes more than just a snapshot to determine who God is. To actually understand who God is and what He can do, you may have to take many different snapshots of Him and patiently put them together to get the whole picture.

If you are not prepared to wait until the end of your story, then you might as well forget about receiving any good thing from the hand of the Lord. Just because things are not, right now, going the way you expected does not mean that you are out of God's will. Just because you have heard "No" so many times from people does not mean that God's answer is "No".

I have discovered in my contact with many highly

successful Christian leaders that most of them have developed such great self-esteem that they refuse to take any rejection personal. If someone says "No", they take it as just a "No" to that day. They will not feel embarrassed at all to return to that same person tomorrow for the same or another request, knowing that that person could change their mind overnight.

One of these men who I have come to very much respect once said that if he had stopped pursuing projects every time someone first said "No", he would not have accomplished anything. The same man also said that he had heard so many "No's" in his fifty years of life that if he were given ten dollars every time someone said "No" to him he would have become a millionaire. The amazing thing is that in spite of the rejections this man experienced he went on to become a multi- millionaire pastor of one of the largest churches in America.

The point is this; if you have been called to represent God in any endeavor, do not allow the passage of time or rejection by people to rob you of the joy of accomplishment. If God spoke to you concerning your assignment, then hold onto that word until it is fulfilled. Be patient and faithful while God is working to set up the right appointments for you. You will never regret the times you took a bold stand for your convictions or patiently waited on the Lord to vindicate you.

One of my favorite scriptures is *Psalm 37:3-5 which says: "Trust in the LORD and do good. Then you will live safely in the land and prosper. Take delight in the LORD, and he will give you your heart's desires. Commit everything you do to the LORD. Trust him, and he will help you" (NLT).*

During the past several years in ministry this Scripture has been a great comfort, encouragement and blessing to Enobong and me. There have been several times when we had to turn to it for comfort and strength while we were waiting for some breakthrough. We have often drawn strength from it while working on projects and waiting for the necessary funds to come in to enable us to pay our bills.

We have turned to this scripture while waiting for healing to manifest in our physical bodies. We turned to it when we were going through some fiery trials of our faith. It was our source of encouragement and strength when dealing with some sensitive administrative issues in the ministry. In every one of these situations we can now testify, to His glory, that it was worth all the waiting we did.

Now let me ask you a question, my friend: How long are you willing to wait to receive your breakthrough? Do you know that sometimes you will have to wait for a long time to generate enough courage and faith to enable you to take on a task? Yes, like the disciples in the boat, you must be willing to exercise patience while trying to steer your boat through your life's storms. Like Peter in *Luke 5* you may have to wait for your Lord to finish giving out the word before your big catch.

So how long are you willing to stand on God's Word and hold unto His promises? Will you stand till the end of your faith? Or will you give up before your victory has manifested? Will you keep standing even after you have done everything you can do in the natural *(Eph.6: 13)*? Or will you cast away your confidence that could be greatly rewarded *(Heb. 10:35)*?

Let me caution that you do not give up on God because He is ultimately coming to your help. Just because it is the third watch of the night does not mean that He has forgotten you. Your salvation is nearer now than when you first began this journey of faith *(Heb. 10:35-39)*. I pray that you do not give up before He arrives to deliver your package.

My prayer is that, like Job, you will be able to proclaim even in your trying situation, *"But as for me, I know that my Redeemer lives, and that he will stand upon the earth at last. And after my body has decayed, yet in my body I will see God"* *(Job 19:25-26).*

GROWTH IN LOVE (Gal. 5:6)

Those who desire to walk by faith or do the impossible must, at the same time, be willing to grow in love. This is because when you make a decision to walk by faith or do the impossible, you will encounter a lot of opposition and misunderstanding. At times Satan will deal you a direct blow. Sometimes he will employ both friends and foes to carry out his dirty work. This opposition will come in spiritual, physical, emotional and human forms. The human opposition may manifest in the form of jealousy, envy, intimidation and persecution. Sometimes it will come in the form of an outright expression of hatred towards you. I have discovered that the most effective weapon of warfare against this sort of opposition is the spiritual force of ***LOVE***.

The Bible does not mention it, but it is possible that in the story in *Matt. 14* the other disciples discouraged or even tried to stop Peter from stepping out of the boat. They may have ridiculed him when he first stepped out of the boat. Perhaps they jeered at him when he began to sink. It is also possible that they became jealous of him after he accomplished this unprecedented feat.

Even if all of these things did happen, none of them would have been a justification for Peter not to love and always extend his goodwill to his brothers. It is actually in situations like these that our maturity in love will be revealed.

Let me also quickly point out that love is more than feeling. Just because someone has an emotional feeling towards a person does not necessarily mean that he loves the person. Some people do that and yet still proceed to take undue advantage of the same people. I have even known some cases in which people sought to harm or even kill people they purported to love and feel for. Behaviors like these go totally against the biblical description of love.

According to the Scriptures, true love is manifested in the way we treat people, especially when they disagree with us. Such love is patient and kind, never jealous or envious, never boastful or proud.

Genuine biblical love is never haughty, selfish or rude. It will never demand having its own way. It is not irritable or touchy. It does not hold grudges and will hardly even notice when others do it wrong. If you love someone you will always be loyal to him *(1 Cor. 13: 4-7 TLB)*. We must operate consistently in this God-kind of love if our faith is to function effectively.

Let me encourage you as I conclude this section not to forget these seven important truths:

1) *Great men and women of faith experience challenges just like anyone else.*
2) *These people are frequently, ordinary people who believe in the extraordinary God.*
3) *When you decide to walk by faith or do the impossible you can expect the enemy to attack you with fear – only don't let it overpower you. Instead remain as bold as the lion.*
4) *Never equate a fall with failure because a fall can open a wide door to growth.*
5) *Don't for a moment assume that because you are in God's will you won't have to wait.*
6) *Always remember that delay is never denial. It may even help you develop patience.*
7) *In the course of walking by faith you will have to take a course on love. Be sure not to fail it.*

YOU CAN DO THE IMPOSSIBLE

PART TWO

ONE STEP AT A TIME

CHAPTER FIVE

ONE STEP AT A TIME: *DAILY TRUST IS ESSENTIAL*

By faith Abraham, when called to go to a place that he would later receive as an inheritance, obeyed and went, even though he did not know where he was going (He. 11: 8).

WITHOUT A POSSIBLE LOGICAL EXPLANATION

How much are you willing to trust in God? Can you trust Him when you cannot give a possible logical explanation for the things taking place in your life? Will you trust Him enough to obey Him when He instructs you to go to a place you do not know? Will you trust and totally rest on His promises, even when you cannot, in the natural, see how He will bring them to pass? Until you are willing to trust Him this way, you will never be able to discover Him.

God's will is to guide us by His Spirit on a daily basis. Unfortunately, most believers don't know this. We usually expect Him to reveal His complete will to us in one giant revelation. We sit around waiting for Him to give us a spectacular revelation of what our whole life is going to be like before we do anything. Don't you ever yield to this common temptation!

Don't sit around waiting for a big and unusual voice. Instead, let God direct you in the little things on a daily basis. You must put to practice what God is saying to you now because it is in small situations that you develop keys to success in bigger things. As you do so, He will show you what adjustments you need to make in your life, what you need to do about specific issues that need to be addressed now, and what you need to leave alone until the proper time *(Eccl. 3: 1)*. I know this to be true not only because of the many scriptures that point to this truth, but also because of my personal experience with God.

Over the years, Enobong and I have received many invitations from God to participate in the faith-walk. These invitations many times came without the revelation of any details of what was going to happen along the way. God usually places a thought in either or both of our hearts. As we stepped out in obedience, He added some more details to the previous instructions.

One example was when I sensed God's prompting to go for theological training in preparation for the ministry to which He was calling me. I did not know what to do at the time. Let me point out here that until you receive a specific instruction from God you need to keep following the last one and the revelation given in His word. Remember that God's word is His will.

Not receiving a specific instruction on what to do, I decided to follow the one in the written word, which says, *"Write my answer (vision) in large, clear letters on a tablet, so that a runner can read it and tell everyone else. But these things I plan won't happen right away. Slowly, steadily, surely, the time approaches when the vision will be fulfilled. If it seems slow, wait patiently, for it will surely take place. It will not be delayed"* (Hab. 2:2-3 NLT).

Based on this injunction from God's word I noted down the vision, prayed about it, and then shared it with close friends and other mature Christians under whom I had submitted myself. I did so knowing that they were going to stand with me in prayer seeking for more directions.

One of those friends was a missionary from the United Kingdom, Miss Mabli Pritchard, who informed me of a Bible college she knew in South Wales in the United Kingdom. She also shared with me the story of another young man for whom God miraculously provided the resources to attend that college.

As I listened to the testimony of how God provided for this man, some faith rose up within me. It suddenly became clear to me that if God could do this for this young man, He would also do the same for me. So I asked Miss Pritchard to contact the college and request the necessary admission material for me. She kindly agreed to do so. When the application materials came, I applied and was accepted to start classes that fall.

WHEN HE ORDERS HE ALSO PROVIDES

As a prospective foreign student, I had to show some evidence of financial support for the period of time I would be studying in the United Kingdom. I had to do this before the school could release the papers I needed to apply for the entry visa into the United Kingdom. This was around June and the classes were to start in September of that year.

Since I did not have such evidence of support, we again prayed and left the matter in God's hand. As we waited on the Lord, He directed Miss Pritchard to write a letter to the college asking them to agree to stand with us in agreement for the Lord to supply all my needs while I would be studying in the United Kingdom. Fortunately, the institution agreed to do so.

Then Miss Pritchard wrote a letter to the British Embassy in Nigeria. In the letter she stated that we did not have physical evidence of financial support to present to the Embassy. She stated, however, that we were trusting in the Lord to provide, through His people, all the support I would need for the three years of study in the United Kingdom. Again, God performed a miracle in this situation and I was granted a six-month entry visa to the United Kingdom. I thanked God for the visa, but I still had to come up with the money for my fare, which in the natural I did not have at the time. I sold absolutely everything I had, but still could not come up with the needed funds.

Nevertheless, I kept praying and trusting the Lord to make a way for me where there was no way in the natural. I continued to believe that He could not have brought me that far to abandon me. That would not be like Him.

GOD STILL MULTIPLIES

With the little I had and a promise from a relative in Lagos, Nigeria to help with some money, my friends organized a simple send-off party for me. A few days later, I proceeded to Lagos en route to the United Kingdom...or so I thought. When I arrived in Lagos, to my utter disappointment, the money that my relative expected to help me with did not come through! The relative told me that he was sorry he could not help as he promised. At this point, I was left with the options of either getting upset and throwing in the towel or pressing on, trusting the Lord to make a way for me. I chose to do the latter.

As I was wondering what to do next, someone who heard about my situation contacted me to inform me of the discount fare that the Nigerian Airways was offering to Nigerian students going abroad. I checked into this program, applied for it, was accepted, and given a 35% discount on the full fare. With this discount I had seventy dollars left to take with me to the United Kingdom to study for three years.

So with a second-hand pair of suit, a winter jacket that some friends had given me, a small suitcase that contained a few items and seventy dollars in traveler's checks, I left Lagos on October 11, 1973 en route to the United Kingdom. At the airport it suddenly occurred to me that I should have bought a gift for the head of the institution that by then had become a friend, despite having never met.

With ten of the seventy dollars I had in my possession I

purchased a gift to present to him upon my arrival. Consequently, I was left with sixty dollars when I boarded the plane to the United Kingdom. Space will not permit me to narrate all the stories of the miraculous provisions that God made for me during the three and a half years stay in Britain. However, I shall share some of those stories to illustrate various points. During those years I watched God miraculously provide for me in ways I would not have imagined when I was in Nigeria. He moved in some people's hearts to pay my school fees anonymously. He also moved in other people's hearts to buy me clothes and give me pocket money for toiletries and books.

One such incident took place during a summer, which I spent with a couple in London. It was getting to the end of the summer and the beginning of another school year. I was beginning to be concerned that the school was about to start and I did not have my fees for the next term. One evening I was so concerned about my situation that I could not concentrate on doing anything. So I decided to go into my room and to cry to the Lord for help. While I was on my knees praying, my host knocked on the door of my room. When I opened the door he informed me that the school just called to say that someone who wished to remain anonymous had just paid my fees in full.

Every time I think of that incident I am reminded of the Scripture that says, *"And it shall come to pass, that before they call, I will answer; and while they are yet speaking, I will hear" (Is. 65:24).* That incident also reminds me of the truth of Paul's instructions in *Philippians 4:6-7* which says, *"Don't worry about anything; instead, pray about everything. Tell God what you need, and thank him for all he has done. If you do this, you will experience God's peace, which is far more wonderful than the human mind can understand. His peace will guard your hearts and minds as you live in Christ Jesus."*

In addition to my personal needs God also, through His people, provided for my then-fiancée to come from Nigeria to the United Kingdom. She came to study in the one-year program offered by the college. A semester before our graduation God provided for us to have a magnificent wedding. Four churches at which we used to minister offered to sponsor the entire wedding. At the time we graduated from the college, all our bills were paid and we had some money left over to meet other personal needs.

HE WILL DO IT AGAIN

After our graduation from the college in Britain we both worked in England for some time. Since then God has relocated us to the United States where we now serve Him in full-time ministry. Here in the United States the Lord provided for both of us to finish our bachelor's degrees. In addition He also provided for me to study for and earn both a Master's degree and Ph.D. in international relations and political science respectively. What a wonderful Provider we serve!

Another example of God's guidance and provision in a similar manner was when we moved from Atlanta, Georgia fifteen years ago to Putnam County in Middle Georgia. We relocated to take the new job that I mentioned in a previous section. Shortly after relocating to Middle Georgia, we began to sense a prompting to start a Bible study. We felt that God wanted us to use the studies to share with the people in this area the concepts of faith that God had taught us through such men as Oral Roberts, Kenneth E. Hagin, Kenneth and Gloria Copeland, Dr. Frederick K. C. Price, the late John Osteen of Lakewood Church of Houston, Texas and many others.

Not knowing all that God was going to do, we obeyed Him. As a result we witnessed many people come to the personal knowledge of Christ as Savior. Many were healed of various kinds of conditions and others were filled with the Holy Spirit with the evidence of speaking in tongues.

A few months after we started teaching the Bible study, my wife and I began to sense a prompting to found The Word of Faith Ministries, Inc. We felt that God wanted us to utilize the Ministry as a vehicle to share with the unreached peoples in other areas, the concepts of faith we had been teaching. Not knowing what to expect, I resigned my new job just a year after I started it. With my wife as a full-time homemaker, I was the only income-earning member of a family of three. My wife was a full-time homemaker at the time.

This is our sixteenth year in this adventure in faith and we still trust Him on a daily basis. One thing that Enobong and I can say is that God has amazed us by the things He has done through The Word of Faith Ministries, Inc. since it was formed on June 20, 1990. By His grace the ministry is operating today with some full-time staff members, some part-time and a number of volunteer staff members.

Over the years we have seen God work through the ministry to touch so many lives from the United States to Africa, Europe, Israel, South America, and the Caribbean. To Him we give all the glory for these wonderful things.

BEYOND OUR WILDEST DREAMS

In spite of our repeated doubts and fears, God has faithfully supplied every need we ever had beyond our wildest dreams. In fact He, many times, provided above our needs so that we had some to put in the storehouse and some left over to help others in need. He has, through the years, demonstrated Himself to be faithful and trustworthy.

God did not always give us the details of what He was going to do, but He always revealed Himself and character whenever it was necessary. We started in 1990 traveling to different parts of the world with the message that faith in God and His word is the answer to every human situation *(Mark 11:23-24).*

The first part of the ministry, to say the least, was very challenging. This was because we had never been in full-time ministry in the United States before. Therefore we were learning everything from the foundation. Things began to change, though, as we traveled to different places ministering to people and building a base of partners and supporters at the same time.

THE ABUNDANT LIFE WORD FELLOWSHIP

By 1992, things had improved considerably and we were beginning to enjoy traveling. Surprisingly, the Lord began to deal with us about cutting down on our travel schedule so that we could concentrate our efforts on developing the ministry in Middle Georgia. We felt that He was telling us to settle down and disciple those we had led to the Lord in this area.

After much prayer and deliberation, we started a daily lunchtime Bible study in our office here in Eatonton, Georgia. This soon grew into our Thursday night Bible study. Later on, the Lord enabled us to obtain a bank loan to purchase some property with a small house and an extremely old singlewide manufactured home. We paid off the loan in less than two years. That, to us, was God's way of encouraging us and confirming the work of our hands *(Ps 90:17)*.

On November 20, 1994 we met in the singlewide manufactured house for the inaugural service of The Abundant Life Word Fellowship – a church that we started as an outgrowth of the The Word Of Ministries, Inc. We used the other house for our children's ministry.

On December 6, 1996 we dedicated a fifty-four hundred square-foot new sanctuary to the glory of God and for our meetings.

I share these personal testimonies only to say that God will not always show you the whole picture when He decides to use you. Yet if you are willing to obey Him from where you are, He will supply the necessary details along the way.

Enobong and I, from our experience during the years, have come to the conclusion that God is faithful to His promises to those that He has called. We also believe that obedience to His call, though difficult at times, always pays off. Finally, we have come to the conclusion that you always end up with more at the end if you are willing to start with the little that you have.

This, we believe, was what the Lord Jesus Christ had in mind when He said to the disciples in *Mark 10:29-30*, *"I tell you the truth, no one who has left home or brothers or sisters or mother or father or children or fields for me and the gospel will fail to receive a hundred times as much in this present age (homes, brothers, sisters, mothers, children and fields–and with them, persecutions) and in the age to come, eternal life."*

WHY NOT GIVE GOD A CHANCE?

If God has invited you to participate in an adventure in faith, I want to encourage you to trust and follow Him, one step at a time. To discover Him and His character you must be willing to trust Him fully. You must be willing to follow His directions even when you do not comprehend the full implication of such obedience.

You must be willing to trust and obey Him even when you don't know the details of how the vision will be fulfilled. That was what Abraham did when God commanded him to leave his country and people and go to some place that he had never been *(Gen. 12:1-2)*. He did the same thing when he was instructed to take a trip to Mount Moriah to sacrifice his only son Isaac *(Gen. 22:1-19)*. To the natural mind such instructions seem quite foolish. But to the man of faith it was yet another opportunity for God to demonstrate His ability to provide grace in times of need *(Gen. 22:7-8)*.

We must always bear in mind that God doesn't do

anything without a reason. We may not fully understand what He may be doing at this time, but it will become clearer as we follow Him on a daily basis *(John 13:7)*. In your daily walk with God He will challenge you to make sacrifices, not just for the sake of the sacrifices. He will sometimes do so to test your willingness to trust and obey Him. The question is: will you be willing to trust and obey him at such critical times in your life?

THE REASONS WHY HE DOESN'T

There are reasons why God generally does not reveal His total program to us. One of the reasons is that He wants us to learn to trust Him even when He does not reveal all the details to us. Another reason is that God knows that if we knew all the details, some parts of it would be too frightening for us to handle. Also, God sometimes withholds some details to prevent us from giving them away to the enemy, who could use it against us.

The most important thing is never whether God reveals the details of His blueprint to us. It is always whether we can trust Him to take care of us during the entire journey. Therefore, if He has called you to any assignment, don't wait for Him to reveal all the details to you because He might not. Instead just trust and obey Him while leaving Him to supply the minute details along the way as you proceed.

CHAPTER SIX

ONE STEP AT A TIME:
YOU MUST YIELD CONTROL

The Lord said to Abram, "Leave your country, your people and your father's house and go to the land I will show you" (Gen. 12:1).

By faith Abraham when called to go to a place he would later receive as an inheritance obeyed and went even though he did not know where he was going (Heb. 11:8).

SIMPLY TRUST

From time to time God calls individuals to take an adventure of faith, not knowing everything to expect. One of the reasons He does not always reveal the full details of the journey is that He wants us to trust Him even when we don't have all the minutiae. Another reason is that most of us would be too terrified to accept His call if we knew everything about the call at the beginning.

In addition, as we pointed out earlier on in the study, some of us would give the information to the enemy who would use it against us. Finally, God generally reveals to us just enough details to get us excited enough to get started. Therefore, when God speaks to you about doing anything for Him, just obey Him. Don't be overly concerned about the part of the process that He doesn't reveal to you now. That will come at the appropriate time.

TRUST - AN IMPORTANT ELEMENT

Trust in God becomes an important element in the obedience process, especially when we remember that some parts of the process will not be as exciting as others. For instance, there may come a time when those who started with you may leave you for various reasons. Some may leave because of some providential circumstance. Others may leave because the organization has outgrown them. Or, as some of them would have you believe, they have outgrown the organization. Some may leave when you feel you most need them, for reasons you may never understand.

For many of you, your best friends who started with you may leave because they honestly believe that you made a turn in the wrong direction. Still others may leave because you have to reluctantly release them. The most important thing is to be careful not to take these situations personal. Rather, trust in God to make it up to you for the losses.

Sometimes the finances may not flow in as fast as you would have liked. At other times it may even seem like you are walking in a pitch-dark tunnel, not knowing where you are, or where you are going. For many of you, there may come a time when your mind and feelings trick you into believing that you did not hear from God when you first started out.

Unless your trust in God is well founded, these are times that Satan can convince you that it is not worth finishing what you started. It is at this point that many lose faith in God, throw in the towel, give up and quit. The question is, will you and I, at such times, hold on to God's unchanging word and trust Him to the end? Unfortunately, so many people waited until they reached the crossroads before confronting this question. You cannot wait until the last minute, though, because then it may be too late. Decide right now that no matter what happens you will take hold of God's grace and press on to the end of the course.

YIELDING THE CONTROL

It can be very frustrating to a believer when he suddenly realizes that neither he nor any other people understand what is going on in his life. Naturally, we all like to feel that we are in control of our lives. We want to feel that we know what we are doing and where we are going. Yet God, with His great sense of humor, has a way of stripping us of our pride so that we can be clothed with His glory.

The Apostle Peter warns us to humble ourselves before the Almighty God that in due time He may exalt us (*1 Peter 5:8*). Our egos always want to hold on to control. However, God gets the glory when we are willing to yield the control.

One thing you must always remember is that God knows what you don't. So don't panic when it seems that you don't know what is going on in your life. Always remember that He does. When it occurs to you that you have used up all your plans, remember that God's plan is still in place. Don't panic when you discover that nothing you do seems to work out the way you expected. Instead just ask Him to institute His plan.

When the numbers on the checkbook don't seem to add up or when the flow of income seems to stop because business is slow or at a standstill, remember that God is still at work in your circumstances and in your life. When you discover that your spouse is throwing away more money into some sinful lifestyle, don't let that frustrate you. Instead, reach out to God more than ever before. Your redemption is nearer now than at any other time in your life.

One of the reasons that the enemy is putting so much pressure on you at this time is that your faith is working. His intention is to exert enough pressure on you that you become discouraged, irritated, frustrated and consequently give up. Nonetheless, if you give a few more pushes, your miracle will be birthed. The frightening part of obedience to God is that you sometimes don't know what He is going to do next or how He is going to do it. The exciting part of it is that whatever He does and however He does it will be the best for you *(Rom.12: 1-3)*.

TURN ON THE PRESSURE

All the present challenges in your life will have no alternative but to bow to God's word. That is, of course, if you patiently apply the appropriate promises of God to your situation *(Jam. 1: 4, Heb. 6: 12)*. The big question is never whether the enemy will yield to God's word. It is always whether you can trust Him to sustain you while you are fighting this good fight of faith *(1 Tim. 6: 12)*.

Let me encourage you, friend, not to give up on God because it is never over until He says so. The good news is that He will not end the fight until you win: that is, if you don't quit. Remain faithful to the call and you will be rewarded at the end.

Friend, as the Word of God says, do not let that "initial happy trust in the Lord die away, no matter what happens". Remember that there is "a reward for those who endure to the end". You need to "keep on patiently doing God's will if you want Him to do for you all that He has promised." Always bear in mind that it is just a matter of time before you see the manifestation of the answers to your prayers. His coming will not be delayed longer than is necessary *(Heb.10: 35-37 TLB)*.

And don't you ever forget that *"those whose faith made them good in God's sight lived by their faith, trusting Him in every situation" (Heb.10: 38TLB)*. He has promised to see us through, if we hold onto our faith to the end. He is never pleased when any of His children turn his back on Him.

My prayer, my friend, is that you do not turn your back on Him and forfeit your breakthrough. I earnestly pray that you may be able to hold on to the end and so receive your promise *(Heb. 10: 35-39 TLB)*.

TOTAL DEPENDENCE

Each challenge we encounter gives us an opportunity to throw our total dependence on God. Each trial provides us with an opportunity to tap into His ability and resources. So don't worry about what God is going to do. Instead, relax, pray, and throw your whole weight on Him *(Phil. 4: 6-7)*. He is strong enough to carry you.

If you believe in an all-knowing, miracle-working God as I do, then step out in total dependence on Him. You will be totally amazed to see what He can do if you are willing to trust Him that much. God is the One you know Him to be when you are closest to Him. The more you are willing to obey Him, the closer you will get to Him *(John 14: 23)*. The closer you get to Him, the more you will discover who He actually is.

No one will ever truly know God until he or she is willing to abandon everything and go out on a limb with Him. To become involved with Him this way requires willingness to leave behind the old traditions, convictions, creeds, philosophies and past experiences that go contrary to His word. Doing so will bring you to that place in your life that nothing is able to separate you from Him or His love *(Rom. 8: 35-39 TLB)*.

A closer walk with God will sometimes demand willingness to get away from the norm and the familiar. This may even involve a change of environment and company, as was the case with Abram in *Genesis 12*. You must come to a point in your life that absolutely nothing is able to come between you and your relationship with God. You are not giving up anything when you are doing it for God and His cause. So give Him all you have and it will pay off in the end.

Furthermore, you must be willing to get so close to God that nothing He does is a surprise to you. It is at this point that you will discover that God is who He says He is. At this point, you will discover the futility of worrying about the future.

Your life must be that of ever-increasing dependence on God and His wisdom *(Jam. 1: 6-7)*. When you come to this place in your walk with God, you will also come to discover how utterly insulting it is to Him when you worry about your future *(Luke 12: 22-32)*. Friend, are you willing to trust Him with the kind of abandonment just described? Are you willing to go so far with Him that if He is not God you will never be able to return? I pray that the lord will help you as you ponder these questions.

CHAPTER SEVEN

ONE STEP AT A TIME: *FEAR – YOUR GREATEST ENEMY*

―──◉──―

By faith Abraham when called to go…obeyed even though he did not know where he was going (Heb. 11: 8).

"I was afraid…and went and hid your talent in the ground. Look there you have what is yours" (Matt. 25: 25).

FEAR – THE GREATEST HINDRANCE TO TAKING BOLD STEPS

In *Matthew 25* our Lord told the story of three servants who were entrusted with different sums of money for investment. Two of them wisely invested and as a result doubled their money. Unfortunately, the third one, being afraid to lose his money, buried it in the ground. When the master returned for an account on their investments, the one who hid his money said, "I was afraid…and hid your talent in the ground." To say the least, the master was furious and asked him why he did not at least invest his money in the bank for the minimum interest. He told the servant that he was not only "lazy" but also "wicked". The master took the money from him and gave it to one of the other servants who invested their money and brought back some interest.

One moral of this story is that God expects a return on His investment in you and me. True, we are not equally talented but He still expects us to use whatever "talents" He has given to us, no matter how little we may think they are. Not having a lot of "talent", to God, is no reason for not being fruitful. Part of fulfilling God's purpose in our lives involves the willingness to risk what He has given us in order to maximize our potential. Avoiding risks and living out of fear hinders us from becoming all that God created us to be. That is why, according to our Lord, this master came down so hard on the unproductive servant. You cannot live your life in fear and expect rewards.

Another lesson to learn from this story is that God will never ask you to do anything that He knew you couldn't do. If He speaks to you about doing something, it is because He knows you are able to perform the task. That is why He will not accept any excuse for not doing what He instructed you to do. So instead of giving excuses, you need to get out and start doing what He instructed you.

Finally, we learn from this parable that if you fail to utilize any opportunity God extends to you, He will take it from you and give it to someone else who will make good use of it. I don't know about you, but it scares me to even think about losing an opportunity because I played around with it. I don't even want to entertain the idea of losing my place among the champions of God's cause because of fear of failure.

DON'T PLAY A ROBBER OR CHEATER

One thing we sometimes fail to realize is that by allowing fear to hinder us from investing our "talents", we usually end up robbing ourselves of the joy of accomplishment. Besides, we also deny those who would have benefited from our investments. So many people get robbed when we fail to pursue our God-given dreams. The good news, though, is that it is not too late to begin investing what God has entrusted to you. If you are not doing so now, you can begin today.

The thing about trusting God on a daily basis is that we must be willing to step out in faith, even in the midst of impossible circumstances. As we have just found out, one of the greatest hindrances to taking bold steps of faith is fear. This can range from fear of failure, criticism and death, fear of men and even fear of making a wrong decision.

In the past I believed that I should never make any moves unless I was absolutely sure of everything involved in such a move. However, I have since come to learn from experience that God will not always reveal certain details to you until you take the first step of obedience to His last command. In fact there will be times when God will trust and even expect you to make certain decisions for Him. He will give you the initial directions but expect you to fill in the details as you proceed. Sometimes God wants you to trust Him while employing the wisdom derived from the written word, your previous experience with Him and the comfort of His Holy Spirit.

HE WILL FIND YOU

There are some moves that God will never make until you initiate them by your obedience. A typical example is when Abraham sent his servant Eliezer to Haran to take a wife for Isaac. Even though Eliezer did not know what to expect he nevertheless proceeded to Haran on his master's instructions. Later on he testified, *"I being in the way the Lord led me to the house of my master's brethren" (Gen. 24: 27).*

I believe that if you are walking in obedience to God and in submission to the proper authorities you should not be afraid to step out in faith. *If you walk with a true and perfect heart before God, He will find you if you ever miss Him.* According to God's word His eyes roam the earth to show Himself strong on behalf of those whose hearts are perfect towards Him *(2 Chron. 16:9).* Does this mean that you must always make perfect decisions before God can bless you? Not at all! Based on this scripture, if you love God with all your heart, keep your motives pure, and submit to the proper authorities over you, then you can expect God to show Himself powerful even in the midst of imperfect judgment calls.

When you don't know what to do in any situation, take some time out to pray. While praying, surrender your will to God and ask Him for wisdom concerning the matter at hand *(Jas. 1: 5)*. Then listen to your heart, step out in faith and follow your heart. Only be sure that your desire is in line with God's word concerning the matter *(Psalm 37: 4)*.

If there is any doubt in your mind after praying, then continue to pray, meantime seeking counsel with more mature Christians. Do not ever make any moves just because you believe you have heard from God. Always be sure that what you have heard is in total agreement with God's word. If you are not sure, verify it with other mature believers.

You can never go wrong following God's written word in any matter. God's word is always His revealed-will *(2 Pet. 1:19-21, 2 Tim. 3: 16-17)*. Therefore, don't be afraid to make decisions as long as they are based on God's word *(John 15:7)*, and mature counsel *(Pr. 24: 5-6 NLT)*.

Don't ever let the fear of not making the right decision stop you from taking steps of faith. You must understand that if you operate under the right authority, walk in love, refrain from strife, and operate with the right motives, God will always protect you in your decision-making. Do not ever be afraid to operate under authority because authorities are there to protect you, not deny you. Yet even if you miss God under those conditions, you can be sure that He will most certainly find you.

So go ahead and seize this opportunity to make that business investment or take your spouse to that expensive restaurant, even if this is going to be a one-time experience! Decide from this moment that henceforth you will take giant calculated risks to try doing things you have never done before. As you practice living this way, you will come to discover that the wider your comfort zone is, the less you will be controlled by fear.

STEPPING OUT IN FAITH

A typical demonstration of how to do the impossible is the story of Peter's walk on the water that we referred to earlier in this book (Matt. 14: 22-33). As you may remember, in the story Peter and the other disciples were struggling in the stormy sea when they saw a person on the water who resembled and sounded like Jesus.

To find out whether indeed it was his Master that he saw walking on the water, Peter asked to be invited to walk on the water with Jesus. He was granted his request. And sure enough, when He stepped out of the boat he was able to walk on the water as long as he was focusing his attention on Jesus.

However, as Peter was walking on the water, he suddenly changed his focus from Jesus to the stormy sea. At that point he began to sink. But, as soon as he realized his mistake he returned his focus to Jesus and called on Him for help. Then Jesus immediately reached out to Peter and walked him to the boat.

One moral of this story is that, *to verify what we see or hear in the spirit we must be willing to risk everything and step out in faith to test what we have heard.* This will involve stepping out of your comfort zone to do something you may have never done before. For some this may involve stepping out to initiate a project, leading a Bible study group, taking a surprise offering in your church for your pastor or even giving a word of prophecy in the Sunday morning church service.

For Peter it involved stepping out of a comfortable boat to walk on the water – something that neither he nor anyone else, except Jesus, had ever done. In the process of stepping out, Peter was able to prove that it was indeed His Master that he saw and His voice that he heard.

Another lesson we learn from this story is that *it is dangerous to focus on the stormy sea (problems) when walking by faith (2 Cor. 14:16-18).* When you step out in faith in answer to God's call, you must remember to keep your focus on Him instead of on the ensuing problems. The easiest way to sink, get drowned or even die is to become so focused on the problems that they overwhelm you.

How many people have had a heart attack by worrying about problems relating to their call instead of continuing to do what God instructed them to do? How many other people have developed other severe medical conditions because of concerns relating to their jobs, families, ministries or businesses?

The third lesson derived from this story is that *it is acceptable to God for you to ask for permission to do what you have never done before.* However, be sure that whatever you want to do is what Jesus is doing or would do.

In other words, don't ever ask Him to give you permission to do anything that is against His will as revealed in His word. If, however, Jesus is doing it or has done it in the past, then you have an absolute right to ask Him to grant you permission to do the same. Let me say it again: it is perfectly all right for you to ask for permission and the grace to win souls for Him, heal the sick, perform miracles and live an abundant and prosperous life just as He did. If you have a desire to do something that is in line with His word, then ask His permission to do it. Not only will He grant your desire, but He also will be there to help you with the needed resources.

The final lesson from this story is that if you ever discover that your focus is misplaced while trying to walk by faith, then you need to set aside your pride and repent. After repenting, you need to call on Him for help even if it means walking you back to the boat. It is sometimes better to go back to the boat and start all over again than try to walk while sinking and almost drowning.

So if you ever sense a call from God to partner with Him, let me again encourage you to step out in faith, obey Him and let Him fill in the details as you walk with Him. I realize that this may sound too forbidding for those people who are used to praying and sitting around waiting for God's confirmations. Let me emphasize, first of all, that there is nothing wrong with seeking confirmation concerning what we may hear or sense in the spirit. I believe that this was what Peter did when he asked Jesus to invite him to walk on the water with Him. Not sure whether it was indeed Jesus speaking to them, Peter requested, *"Lord, if it's you, tell me to come to you on the water (Matt. 14:28 NIV)"*. In response Jesus said, *"Come."*

However, I have also noticed that many of those claiming to be waiting for signs or confirmations from God are actually using this as an excuse for inaction. These people sit around doing nothing but worrying about the fact that their situations might become worse. Let's not forget, though, that focusing on and worrying about problems don't resolve them *(Matt 6: 27)*. They make them even worse in many instances. What usually brings a change to any situation are courageous and bold actions based on God's word and the prompting of God's Holy Spirit. Yet someone may ask, "What if I miss God?" Then welcome to the family. We all at some point missed God but He found us. And just as he found us, He also will do the same for you.

THE RIGHT, PRIVILEGE AND THE POWER OF CHOICE

Two of the most potent weapons that God has given to His children are the weapons of choice and decision-making. In fact, for the most part, your present position in life is the result of the totality of your past decisions and choices.

The powers of choice and decision-making are incredibly potent tools in each person's hand. If employed properly, you can use them to defeat the devil in every contest. If these tools are misused, the devil can win in every contest you engage in with him. With the right use of these tools you can accomplish great things for God. Their misuse can rob you of the potential to be effective for Him. The choice is yours as to how you employ these powerful tools that God has handed to you.

GETTING READY FOR THE NEXT LEVEL

Some people purporting to wait for a word from God will never receive one. One reason is that they have not yet acted on the last word that they received from God. They are too terrified to do anything that involves risks or sacrifices. The fact is that they are not yet ready for that next level of walk with God. They are waiting for the perfect conditions, which will never occur. If you are one of such people I want to refer you to Solomon, the wisest man that has ever lived. According to Solomon, *"If you wait for perfect conditions, you will never get anything done. God's ways are as mysterious as the pathway of the wind, and as the manner the human spirit is infused into the little body of a baby while it is yet in his mother's womb"* (Eccl. 11: 4-5 TLB). Summing up, Solomon advised, *"Keep on sowing your seed, for you never know which will grow – perhaps it all will"* (Eccl. 11: 6 TLB).

If you are one of those just described I want to encourage you to step out of your comfortable position. Don't be afraid to try something that you have never done before. Realize that you may never have the perfect condition that you are waiting for *(Eccl. 11: 4)*. You will always have to face a measure of risk whenever you decide to step out of your comfortable position. The good thing, though, is that the more you are willing to take such risks the wider your comfort zone will expand.

God can do anything except make decisions for you. He has provided you with the privilege, the authority and the choice to use His word, His Son's Name, His own Spirit, and His own authority as your weapons. What more do you need to enable you to do something for God? Utilize these powerful tools and He will back you up with all His power *(Mk. 16: 15-20)*.

NO NEED FOR A SPECIAL REVELATION.

Right now some of you reading this book strongly believe that God is speaking to you about serving Him in some capacity. There is something you strongly believe God is asking you to do. Why not test what you've heard by praying and stepping out in obedience, a little bit at a time? The only confirmation you need is the prompting in your heart that has already been confirmed by God's written word. Let me encourage you to abandon your fears and self-doubts and step out in faith and trust Him to guide you to the next step.

Don't wait for a special revelation before you pray for the sick. Just find them out, pray for them and watch them recover according to God's written word *(Mk. 16: 15-20)*. Don't wait for a special word before reaching out to and pointing sinners to Jesus as the Savior. You don't need a special revelation to do the so-called impossible or great things for God. All you need is a humble disposition, a willingness to risk your reputation, and a simple faith in an extraordinary God. So step out a little at a time. Declare your intentions and put some action to it! Then God will do for you according to your faith *(Matt. 9: 29)*.

YOU CAN DO THE IMPOSSIBLE:

PART THREE

LIVING WITH GOD'S PURPOSE IN MIND

CHAPTER EIGHT

LIVING WITH GOD'S PURPOSE: *DISCOVER YOUR PURPOSE*

In many ways the earth is a junk pile upon which are heaped human beings who fail to find their place and who are unfulfilled and disillusioned. Oral Roberts

Look carefully then how you walk! Live purposefully and worthily and accurately, not as unwise and witless...Make the very most of time (buying up each opportunity), because the days are evil (Eph. 5:15-16).

IMPORTANT QUESTIONS TO CONSIDER

Plato one of the pioneers of philosophy said that an unexamined life is a useless life. Unfortunately, many lives are unexamined. Because some people have never stopped to examine their lives, they end up not making the most out of the potential they have.

Have you ever stopped to ask yourself such questions as, "Why am I here?" "Why did God place me on this earth?" "Is there a purpose for my life? Or am I a product of chance?" "Am I here on a mission? Or do I just exist to make a living?" These are very important questions to consider. Unfortunately, few people ever pause to consider them.

One thing I have discovered from my studies and personal walk with God is that the faith-walk or doing the impossible is natural for those who are working out God's purpose in their lives. It is in fact impossible to successfully undertake a genuine faith–walk without the knowledge and understanding of God's purpose for one's life.

As someone has well put it, "People who fulfill their calling exude excitement and connection to their gifts that transcends fame...Money never replaces purpose. When you find that thing you'd do for free you've probably found your calling". I want to add here that when you discover your calling it will become for you a stepping-stone to doing the impossible.

The very knowledge of the fact that you are fulfilling God's purpose will generate in you more faith in God and His word that nothing else can. Knowing that you are on course to fulfilling God's assignment will generate more courage and strength for you to continue during difficult times than nothing else will. This is why no one should contemplate undertaking the impossible or faith-walk unless he or she has a clear understanding of the specific purpose of God for his or her life.

Discovering and walking in the purpose of God must be the primary occupation of every individual. When you discover and set out to fulfill the purpose of God, He will supply the grace, strength, faith and the other needed resources to do what is humanly impossible.

So many people live their lives struggling from one day to the next because they have not yet discovered God's purpose and plan for their lives. They take whatever life deals out to them, going along and getting along with any and everything that comes until they discover one day that their lives have spun out of control. For many people such discovery was made when it was too late to make any adjustments. How easy it is to let our lives get out of control!

Paul, realizing this, warned the believers in *Eph. 5:16* to live with purpose in mind, making the most of their time. I wonder whether this is the way you live your life – making the most of your time. If not, then why not? Maybe it's time to pause and examine your life. I believe that one of the most potent and propelling forces on the universe is the spiritual *force of purpose*.

What a different world it would be if every person took time to search, discover and fulfill his purpose! Wouldn't it be wonderful if every one were motivated to live in the light of God's purpose instead of by chance?

Unfortunately, most people just drift along life with no reason or purpose. They drift along without any plan or direction. No wonder then, the world is full of so many miserable, angry and therefore dangerous people. These are people who always regret the fact that they missed opportunities. They are the ones that see no meaning in life and are never able to get ahead in any aspect of life.

Hopefully, the above description does not fit you. But for anyone that is reading this book that fits this description, I have good news for you. You don't have to drift along always feeling angry and miserable. You can discover God's purpose for your life, live in the light of this purpose and be happy and thankful all the time *(Col. 1:9-12)*.

DISCOVERING GOD'S PURPOSE

Most people that I know want to discover and fulfill God's purpose for their lives. At the same time, I have also found out that many of these people don't know how to discover God's purpose for their lives. Consequently, they drift along taking whatever comes. It's possible, though, to discover specifically what God created you for.

1. KNOW YOUR GOD

The ***first step*** to discovering your purpose in life is to **know the One who created you**. Unfortunately, many people go to the wrong people to find out their purpose. They fail to realize that the only person who knows the purpose for which a thing was created is the person who created it. In the same way, the only person who knows the purpose for which you were created is the One who created you.

Writing to the Ephesians, Paul reminded them that believers in Christ are: *"God's (own) handiwork (His workmanship), recreated in Christ Jesus, (born anew) that they may do those good works which God predestined (planned before), for them, taking the paths which He prepared ahead of time that they should walk in them (living the good life) which He prepared and made ready for them to live"* (Eph. 2:10 Amp.).

It is clear from the above scripture that God created us for a purpose. It is also clear that God has a plan of good life for His children and that those who discover and function in His purpose enjoy this good life that God planned for them. Someone reading this book may be wondering, "But how can I know God in a personal way, so that I can discover and function in the purpose for which He created me?" The answer to this question is that you come to a personal knowledge of God by establishing a personal relationship with His Son Jesus Christ.

"But how do I establish an intimate relationship with Jesus?" you may ask. The answer is, by recognizing that He died for you and then accepting Him as your Savior. When you establish a relationship with God through His Son Jesus Christ, and as you spend time with Him, then God will reveal to you the purpose for which you were created. Until then, God's purpose for you will be hidden and illusive.

2. *KNOW YOURSELF*

The **_second step_** to discovering God's purpose is to **_know yourself._** The personal knowledge of God is the most important factor in the process of discovering your purpose. Equally important, however, is the fact that you know yourself if you truly desire to know your true purpose in life.

One of the greatest mistakes that people make is to spend most of their lives trying to be someone they know, because they don't know themselves. Therefore, I want to re-emphasize here the importance of knowing and understanding yourself in order to discover and fulfill your purpose.

You must know and understand those factors that influence your life. You must know what your temperament is so that you can know why you act the way you do. You must recognize that you are unique and there is only one person like you and that's you.

You must know that you are beautifully and wonderfully made in spite of your natural strengths or weaknesses. If you don't understand these facts you will spend most of your life trying to be someone that you are not and end up being nobody at all.

One good thing about knowing yourself is that such knowledge will enable you to change or at least monitor whatever needs to be controlled. By monitoring and controlling some factors you can minimize your weaknesses while at the same time maximizing your strengths. Identifying and monitoring the things that influence your behavior, both your baggage and your primers, will enable you build steps that will lead to fulfilling the purpose for which God created you.

3. KNOW YOUR DESIRES

The **_next step_** to discovering your purpose is to **_know your desires_**. God works through our desires and passions. Desires are the things that you want for your life. Passions are the things that consume your interest and time.

Contrary to popular belief, it is God that places in us the right and healthy desires for a better future. Otherwise, why would He promise to give us the desires of our hearts? In *Psalm 37:4,* for example, the Bible tells us that if we delight ourselves in the Lord, He will give us our heart's desires. Also, in *Philippians 2:12-13* the Apostle Paul reminds us that it is God who works in us to place both the desires and the ability to fulfill them.

Godly desires and passions are God's tools to enable us discover and fulfill His will for our lives. They are instruments that He uses to enable us release the potential He placed in us.

Some people are afraid to ask God to reveal their purpose in life. They fear that God might force them to do something they don't desire to do if they yield to His will. Unfortunately, this is one of the biggest lies employed by Satan to stop God's people from pursuing God's will for their lives.

It is actually God who puts good and healthy desires for excellence in our hearts. I believe that the person who said that God has a hard enough time trying to get people to do the good things they desire, than to waste His time trying to force them to do things they don't want to do, was right.

4. KNOW YOUR PASSIONS

The *fourth step* to discovering God's purpose is to *know your passions.* As I explained earlier, your passions are the things that consume your interest, time and energy. For instance, what are the things you love to do? What are the things that you hate? What are the things that make you cry? What are the things that make you laugh? These are some of the things that most people pay very little attention to. Yet in fact these are not the things to take lightly or ignore.

Did you know that what you love to do might actually reveal your gifting? That what you hate may reveal what God created you to correct? That what makes you cry may actually reveal what you were created to heal? ***Don't ever undermine those passions and emotions.*** They may be pointers to the reason that you are here.

5. KNOW YOUR PRIMARY AND SECONDARY GIFTS

The *final step* to discovering God's purpose for your life is to *know your gifs.* Your gift is the particular "talent" or "talents" that God endowed you with when you were born.

They are not only what you love to do, but also what you are good at. Your gift is what enables you to be productive. God gave you these gifts to enable you to fulfill His purpose. It will produce something that will meet others' needs and therefore cause you to become a blessing to them.

I believe that my gift is the ability to utilize words. Over the years God has enabled me to use this gift to touch and impact many lives. God has enabled me, over the years, to employ both written and spoken words to influence many in the right direction. Those who know me in person know that talking and writing is no problem for me.

Listen, my friend, just like me there is something that God placed in you at birth to enable you to fulfill His purpose. Find out what your primary gift is and focus most of your attention on developing it.

Your primary gift is God's major tool to enable you release your God-given potential. Your other gifts are to supplement and support your primary gift. Therefore, be sure not to become so distracted by your secondary gifts that you neglect to develop your primary gift.

I personally love to make a joyful noise to the Lord on the drums from time to time. I am always careful, however, to make sure that my love for the drums does not interfere with my call to teach the word of God. It is quite easy to spend so much time trying to improve my drum-playing skills that I fail to spend enough time preparing for the teaching of the word. So I constantly work hard to remind myself that drum playing is a hobby but teaching the word of God is an assignment.

Your primary gift will enable you to fulfill God's purpose. It will make you happy and fulfilled. The more you develop and utilize it, the more its utility will open other doors for you. Your primary gift, if properly employed, should bring enough resources to enable you to fulfill God's purpose for your life. As a result, you will remain a continuous blessing to God's Kingdom, your family and, other people that God will bring into your life. Other gifts are just supplements to your primary gift.

The Bible informs us that a man's gift will open doors to royalty for him. *(Prov. 18: 16)*. Let me encourage you to go to work to find out what your primary gift is. When you discover it, spend time to develop it until you are good at it. As you do so, God will use the gift to open doors of service for you and that of being a blessing to others.

YOU ARE NOT A PRODUCT OF AN ACCIDENT

Let me emphasize again, friend, that God created you for a purpose. It does not matter how or where you were born. You are very valuable to God who created you.

To discover and fulfill God's purpose you must know your God, know yourself, know your desires, know your passions and finally know your gifting. Without the knowledge and thorough understanding of these factors that influence your life, it will be difficult for you to discover and fulfill your purpose. When you exit this world, be sure that you have given to it all that God sent you to deliver.

CHAPTER NINE

LIVING WITH GOD'S PURPOSE: *ESTABLISH A STRONG SPIRITUAL FOUNDATION*

⋆⇒◯⇐⋆

For this purpose the Son of man was manifested that He might destroy the works of the devil. (1 John 5:8)

GOD'S PURPOSE – THE REASON FOR LIVING.

Sometime ago I heard a story about a Christian who was asked, as he was dying, whether he had any regrets concerning any aspect of his long life. His answer was that he did have one. When asked what it was, he replied that, after many years as a Christian, he was coming to the end of his life without having won a soul for the Lord.

Unfortunately, this man had to wait until the end of his life to realize that he was not fulfilling the one purpose for which God had created and saved him. Maybe one reason he failed to fulfill his purpose was that no one took time to properly instruct him on the power of purpose. Unfortunately, he also failed to take time to search for and discover the truth himself. However, it wouldn't surprise me to find that this same man probably devoted his life to the pursuit of other things, which did not have anything to do with the actual call of God on his life.

Sad to say, but the man's story represents that of millions of men and women all over the world. These people float around in life taking anything that life deals out to them. They hope that whatever will be will be, only to discover at the end of their lives that nothing significant took place within it. They were busy, but not in their Lord's business. They attended church as a ritual and paid their tithes as a duty but never actually took time to find out what they were here for. They never took time to form, let alone establish, a strong spiritual foundation for their lives. To them, the winning of souls and the propagation of the gospel belonged to the pastor's domain.

To these folks, their responsibility was to go to church so that they would feel good and from time to time exchange handshakes with other folks in the church. Such people end up especially miserable and frustrated at the end of their lives.

Thank God for some dying people who can look back on their lives with thanks and gratitude to God. They know that they will exit this life thankful that they lived their lives to the fullest and with God's purpose in view. Consequently, they are very fulfilled, having known that they had accomplished what they were here for. They will die knowing that their lives impacted and made significant difference in the lives of others.

Regrettably, many others like the man we mentioned will come to the end of their lives not able to enjoy such fulfillment. The reason is that they lived their lives without God's purpose in view. Their lives were driven not by God's purpose but by their selfish ambitions, passions and desires.

They lived for themselves rather than make their lives count by serving others with the talents and the abilities that God gave them. As a result, they ended up becoming disillusioned and frustrated. They had nothing to show at the end of their lives. All that they will be remembered for is that they were born, lived and died without ever discovering, let alone fulfilling, God's purpose for their lives.

THE BIG QUESTION

The big question for every one of us at the end of our lives will not be how long we lived here on earth. It will be: Did you discover God's purpose and deliberately execute it the best way you understood it while you were on earth?

You don't want it said at the end of your life that you were born, lived to make a living, married, had children and died without discovering the real purpose God had for you. You want to be remembered for having fulfilled the mission and the assignment God specifically designed for you. You are not here to make a living; you are here on a mission.

You want to be remembered for having been a solution rather than a problem. You were designed to provide answers to the needs in people's lives rather than drain the life out of everyone who comes your way. When you use your life for anything other than what you were created for, you stink. If you don't discover God's purpose for your life and fulfill it, you will hate, abuse and eventually destroy yourself.

Purpose is the reason for which anything was created. It is the most dynamic spiritual force in any person's life. Without purpose there is no need for existence. God is the God of plan, design and purpose. He created every one of us to fulfill a specific purpose. He has a plan for your life. Find out His purpose and plan for your life and fulfill them and you will be happy the rest of your life. If you miss your purpose in life you will end up becoming the most miserable creature on earth, no matter how much wealth you posses.

Sometime ago I knew a man who was a multi-millionaire. The only problem with this man was that he lived his life just to make money. He devoted his entire life to making all the money he could and then canned all the money he made. Now there is nothing wrong with making money, as long as you realize that money is a tool to enable you fulfill the purpose of God. There is everything wrong, though, with living to accumulate all the wealth you can and canning all of it. There is something wrong with just making money and not enjoying it, which is what this man did.

Eventually, this multi-millionaire died miserably in a run-down and depleted house. He rode around the city he lived in a car that could barely transport him to where he was going. It makes you wonder whether this was God's perfect will for this man and his family. I don't believe it was. On the contrary, I believe that God made the man wealthy so that he could enjoy the fruit of his labor with his family, use part of his wealth to support God's work and other people that God would send into his life, and leave some of that wealth to his children and grandchildren.

I know a number of other multi-millionaires who are doing just that, and I have watched God continue to bless them over the years. One time we had lunch with one of such men. During the lunch we asked him why he continued to work so hard when he could have just retired, relaxed, and then begin to spend what he had. His reply was that he wanted to see how much money he could give away to good causes and still remain a multi-millionaire. It is very important that you search for, discover and fulfill God's purpose for your life. If not, you will end up as a big problem, not only for yourself, but also for everyone else around you.

ESTABLISH A STRONG SPIRIUAL BASE

Let me reassert that before seeking to discover your purpose you must know the One who created you. In addition, you must know yourself. You know yourself by knowing your passions, your natural gifting and the spiritual gifts with which God has endowed you. Your spiritual and natural gifts are not products of chance or accident. They were designed by God to help you fulfill His purpose and assignment on this earth.

Before searching for your purpose, be sure to establish a strong spiritual foundation on which to build your life. This is important because you will need a strong spiritual undergirding to effectively fulfill God's purpose for your life. Get to know the God of the Bible through His Son Jesus Christ. With His word, develop a strong spiritual foundation upon which to base your life.

Live your life with the fulfillment of God's purpose as the most important driving force. Don't just live to make a living because you are here on a mission. Living your life with God's purpose in mind is one thing that will put you on your way to being able to achieve what is naturally impossible. It will fuel your desire to succeed, inject passion into your life and give you reason to keep going when the going gets tough.

CHAPTER TEN

LIVING WITH GOD'S PURPOSE:
TAKE TIME TO DEVELOP YOUR LIFE VISION

After Lot was gone, the Lord said to Abram, "Look as far as you can see in every direction, for I am going to give it all to you and your descendants"(Gen. 13:14-15 TLB)

DEVELOP YOUR LIFE'S VISION

With your knowledge of God, yourself, and all the other factors mentioned, you must **develop a vision of a better future** if you truly desire to fulfill God's purpose for you. Purpose is the reason for which you were created. *A vision is an inner picture of where you believe God is taking you.* It is the inner picture of where you passionately desire to be.

A vision provides you with *direction and motivation*. It provides the reason to live from one day to the next. A vision paints on the canvas of your heart the picture of how God can use you to create a better future for you and for others.

A vision fuels your passion and provides the reason for existence. Without a vision people are unrestrained. However, a vision provides discipline and a parameter for action and behavior. Until you develop your life's vision, you will be a Jack-of-all-trades and a master of nothing *(Prov. 29:18).*

THE GOD OF DESIGN, PLAN, AND PURPOSE

Developing a life's vision is one of the most difficult tasks for many people. Many people live their lives without a plan and a vision of what they would like for their lives. They just take whatever life deals out to them, whether good or bad. Yet this is not God's best for His people. His best for His children is that they enjoy their lives because they have discovered and carefully followed His plan and purpose for them.

A careful study of the God of the Bible clearly indicates that ***He is the God of design, plan and purpose.*** He designed your life to fit His purpose for you, just as the architect designs a house to fit its purpose. To live a life not based on careful, prayerful, and consciously planned decisions is an indictment on our faith. However, to carefully plan our lives, we must know where we are heading to.

It is the vision from God that provides the roadmap that makes it possible for us to know where we are going. May I ask you, friend, is your present life directed by the passion fueled by God's purpose and God-given vision? Or is your life directed by chance and whatever life deals out to you? Your answers to these questions are important and will determine what will be said about you when you exit this life.

PUT YOUR IMAGINATION TO WORK

One of the most powerful gifts given to man is the power of imagination. With it God can work miracles in any life *(Eph. 3:20)*. Without it you can be stuck in one position forever. That is why you must put your imagination to work. See yourself beyond your present condition.

Don't be discouraged or intimidated by your present condition in life. Instead be very thankful to God for how far He has brought you and, keep your focus on where you are going. The old adage that what you see is what you get is, to some extent, quite true. That is why God said to His friend Abraham, ***"Look as far as you can see in every direction,***

for I am going to give all to you and your descendants" *(Gen.13: 14-15 TLB).*

God said to Joshua when he was given the assignment of conquering the strongest city in the Promised Land, ***"See, I have delivered Jericho into your hands, along with its king and fighting men"*** *(Josh. 6: 2 NIV).* God was telling Joshua that if he could envision the defeat of the king of Jericho and his army, then it would be so.

This is a spiritual principle, which will apply in every situation. If you can believe and see it, you can have it. This is a two-edged sword that works efficiently. It works for both negative and positive visions.

Unfortunately, many people are exceptionally good at envisioning negative things happening to them and they usually experience them. Nonetheless, such people can turn their negative faith into a positive one. They need to employ the same energy to imagine and believe for positive and good things for their lives. If they do, it will happen to them according to their faith.

I had a friend who was afraid that he might have cancer and die young simply because his mother and sister died young. At the age of fifty he had a massive heart attack and later on he was diagnosed with cancer. Even though the doctors gave him very little chance to live he, nevertheless, decided that he was not going to die.

My friend had a little boy that he did not want to leave behind for someone else to raise. To bolster his faith he copied on index cards all the healing portions in the Bible that he could find. He then memorized these scriptures and quoted each of them several times a day. He did so to paint on the canvas of his mind the picture of health and healing.

Today the same doctors who gave my friend no chance to live because he refused to take chemotherapy treatment are surprised at the dramatic turn around in his health. My friend had utilized the power of imagination to paint the picture of health on the canvas of his heart. He did so by utilizing God's promises concerning healing. Do you know what? I actually believe that if my friend had utilized the scriptures, before he had the cancer, the way he did after the diagnosis of the disease, he might not have had the cancer in the first place.

Listen, my friend, your imagination is an extraordinarily powerful tool to enable you fulfill the purpose of God in your life. Make sure that you utilize it to the maximum for your benefit. *Always bear in mind that before God delivers it to you, you must first see it in your spirit.*

Let me ask you a question, friend. Who do you see at the end of your life? What would you like for people to say about you during your eulogy? You must define this image and make it clear, if you desire to see God's purpose fulfilled in your life. If you cannot clearly define and see this image, you might as well forget about fulfilling your destiny in life.

TAKE OFF THE LIMITS

As a final note, let me encourage you, in formulating your vision, to take off all barriers and limitations to your dream. In formulating your vision see something that is much bigger than your upbringing and your parental or racial background, your educational achievement, or no achievement. Your God is bigger than all of these things put together.

In other words, don't limit yourself by natural barriers when formulating a vision for your life. There is great danger in limited visions. One of the problems is that you may hit the ground if your target is too low. Therefore, aim so high that even if you miss by a few inches, you won't shoot too low.

If you are a young person, imagine yourself beyond gang membership and the streets. See yourself as a college graduate; see yourself in business, in pulpit ministry, in practice as a medical doctor or lawyer. Picture yourself receiving an award for writing a bestseller.

See yourself as a carpenter, electrician or a nurse making useful contribution to your community. Envision God using you to bless and change peoples' lives. *__You can invest in people instead of draining from them.__* You can be a blessing instead of a curse. You can be a pacesetter, a barrier-breaker, a model, a sign and a symbol, a source of God's blessing and a strong witness for Christ.

Did you know that most of those in solitary confinements and prisons all over the world had limited visions? Yes, they did. Believe it or not, many of these men and women, young and old, whose lives are wasting away in jails and prisons today, had limited visions.

Many of these people had vowed that no one was going to run their lives and no one was going to control them. The sad thing is that these are the very people who end up in these institutions where they are not only controlled, but everything they do is what they are told to do.

So as you formulate your vision, foresee beyond your immediate environment. See yourself becoming something much bigger than anything you have so far experienced in life.

That's how you will get to fulfill God's purpose for your life.

Dr. Ben Carson, one of the top neurosurgeons in the world, started in hostile environments in Detroit and Boston. Like many young black men, Dr, Carson had an incredibly difficult childhood. He grew up in abject poverty, started with a dreadfully bad temper and poor grades in school. A single mother who merely had a third grade education raised him.

He grew up in gang-infested neighborhoods and at one time almost killed a friend when he tried to stab him over a minutely significant thing. After that incident, according to Dr Carson, with God's help and his mother's determination, he decided to change his vision from that of becoming a gangster to that of becoming someone who could be of help to others.

He made a quality decision from that time to cultivate self-motivation, patience, understanding and most of all to renew his faith in God. As a result, his grades in school changed. He graduated with a GPA high enough to obtain scholarships to college. He maintained grades that enabled him get into medical school.

Today, in spite of his upbringing and initial handicaps, Dr. Carson is the Director of Pediatric Neurosurgery at John Hopkins Medical Center in Baltimore, Maryland. He has held this position since 1984 when at the age of 33 he became the youngest person to head a major division in John Hopkins Medical Center.

Today, the young man who began his life as a gangster is known all over the world. He is known, not because of his criminal history, but for his many contributions to pediatric neurosurgery. If Dr. Carson could do it, there is no reason you could not rise above your limitations to become whatever God has planned for you.

GOD'S WORD - THE ONLY LIMIT

As a believer in Christ, you can dream about anything that God promises in His Word *(Ps. 127:1-2)*. God has obligated Himself to deliver whatever He promises in His word. His will for you are very clearly spelled out in His **Word** *(1Jn 5:14-15)*.

Jesus said: *"If you stay in me and obey my commands, you may ask any request you like and it will be granted" (John 15:7)*. So be sure as you formulate your vision that you don't see anything that goes against what God promises in His Word.

As long as you remain within the confines of God's word you can count on God's provision and His protection. Outside of God's word, you are on your own and should not expect God to provide for, let alone protect, you.

It is sometimes enormously tempting to go after things that are contrary to God's commands and promises because they look attractive. Nonetheless, if you are ever tempted to ignore God and His command, do resist that temptation *(1Pet. 5:8-9)*. If you don't, you will pay an awfully high price for your decision.

BUILD YOUR LIFE ON GOD'S WORD

Build your life upon God's Word and you won't have to worry about the pending storms *(Matt. 7:12-14, 21-27)*. God's word is the strongest spiritual base upon which to build your life.

Always remember that there are no shortcuts to lifelong success *(Prov. 28:18)*. Each successful person you know had to pay a price to get there. Therefore be ready to pay whatever price it takes to get your life strongly founded on the word.

Be ready to pay any price to learn and put the word to practice. Be a doer of the word and not a hearer only, deceiving yourself.

If you compromise your deeply held values to obtain anything, you will eventually pay a high price for the decision. This again is the reason you must develop that strong spiritual foundation based on God's eternal truth.

A strong spiritual base will provide for you discipline, a parameter for your actions, inner peace, and restraint when needed. It will also provide the incentive to treat others, as you would like to be treated *(Matt. 7:12)*.

NEVER CUT OFF VITAL RELATIONS

As you formulate and develop your vision of a better future, you must be careful to maintain all vital relationships. Many people blindly pursue things they know will cut them off from vital relationships such as with God, His people, their family or friends who truly love and care for them. Don't do that! You may not realize today how important these relationships are, but I promise you that you will need them later on in your life.

The Lord Jesus, addressing the disciples in *Mark 8:36* asked the question: ***"What shall it profit a man if he gains the whole world, and loses his own soul?"*** He was asking them what good it was to have the entire world and all it offers and then at the end forfeit some of the most important things in life.

Don't you know of people who spent most of their lives pursuing something only to discover at the end that there was no one for them to enjoy it with? Let me caution you again that you never isolate yourself from God, your family or your genuine friends. If you do, you will certainly regret it at the end of your life.

Let me also remind you again as I conclude this chapter to get to know God in a personal way through His Son Jesus Christ. Then discover your God-designed purpose by knowing your spiritual and natural gifts, your desires and passions. Employ your knowledge of God and yourself to formulate a vision of a better future for yourself and your community.

Put your imagination to work. Begin from the end and come back to where you are now. Formulate for you an unlimited vision based on God's Word. ***See beyond your present environment to something bigger and better than anything you have ever experienced.*** Only be sure that in formulating your vision you take God, your family and genuine friends with you. If you follow these simple guidelines you certainly will live a fulfilled life. This is exactly what it means to live with a mission in view instead of just surviving to make a living.

CHAPTER ELEVEN

LIVING WITH GOD'S PURPOSE: *THE MOST IMPORTANT DRIVING FORCE*

God placed us on this earth to accomplish a certain number of things. Right now I am so far behind I will never die. —- Anon.

GOD'S PURPOSE MUST BE THE MOST IMPORTANT DRIVING FORCE IN LIFE

Purpose! What is it? It is the reason for which anything was created. It is the only legitimate reason for existence. Purpose ought to be the most important driving force in any person's life. Every person was born into the world for a specific purpose. You are not a human doing, but a human being. No person should engage in any task without first finding out the purpose for which he was created.

Taking on any task without first discovering the purpose for one's life will be making a big mistake. Anyone doing this will be wasting his time, which is one of the most valuable resources entrusted to us. Pursuing any course in life other than God's purpose for you will result in frustration and despair. Unfortunately, too many people find this out too late. You don't want to be one of these people.

FINDING TRUE MEANING IN LIFE

Too many people, regrettably, go around in a circle supposedly looking for meaning in life. The only way to find true meaning in_life, is to discover and fulfill God's purpose for you.

Purpose will give you something for which to live. In

fact, all truly fulfilled people are purpose-driven. All truly successful and fulfilled attorneys, doctors, ministers of God's word, cleaners, builders, architects and so forth are purpose-driven.

Purpose is one of the most powerful spiritual forces in your life. It must become the most powerful driving force in the lives of those who desire to steer in the right course of life. Finding out the purpose for which God created you and working diligently to fulfill it will make you one of the happiest and most fulfilled people on the earth.

Some people erroneously believe that by spending time pursuing money and fame they will ultimately be happy. There is nothing further from the truth than this. The truth is that some of the most miserable and unfulfilled people on earth are some of the richest. While money with the knowledge of God can be a useful tool for service and happiness, money without God can become the source of some of the greatest problems one would ever encounter.

So stop going after money and fame. Begin right away to seek to discover your purpose, and when you discover it, pursue it passionately. As you do so, money with fame will be the natural result. When you discover your purpose in life and pursue it with passion, you will be surprised how many doors of opportunities will be opened to you.

RELEASING YOUR POTENTIAL

You must discover your purpose to be able to do anything of significance. It is impossible to do anything of eternal value unless you discover your purpose in life. Before you engage in any activity, first find out who you are, because who you are is closely tied to your purpose in life.

Discovering who you were made to be will bring you success and fulfillment. Consequently, you will also be able to bring joy, peace, and fulfillment to others. Although hard work is an essential requirement to becoming truly successful, true success is much more than just hard work.

True success involves employing your God-given abilities to fulfill God's purpose for you. Utilizing your abilities for God' purpose will help to create a better world for others as well as a better future for you.

GOD REVEALS YOUR POTENTIAL

As I mentioned earlier in the study, to discover your true purpose, you must come to a personal knowledge of the God who created you. You must know God as your Creator, Redeemer, Defense, and Source. This is because it's only God who can reveal to you the purpose for which you were created. Moreover, you must know Him through a personal relationship with His Son Jesus Christ.

Remember what Paul wrote to the Ephesians? He said, *"For we are God's (own) handiwork (His workmanship), recreated in Christ Jesus (born anew), that we may do the good works which God predestined (planned beforehand), for us (taking paths which He prepared ahead of time), that we should walk in them (living the good life which He prearranged and made ready for us to live) (Eph. 2:10 Amp).*

In essence God prearranged a good and successful life for us. However, you can only begin to experience this life when you enter into a personal relationship with Him through His Son Jesus Christ. First you must acknowledge that you are a sinner, separated from God, not only by your sins, but also by your sin nature. Secondly, you must ask God to forgive your sins because His Son died for you. Finally, you must invite Jesus to come into and rule your life.

God's Spirit, speaking through John, said, *"Here I am! I stand at the door and knock. If anyone hears my voice and opens the door, I will come in and eat with him, and he with me" (Rev. 3:20NIV).*

POSITIVE AND NEGATIVE INFLUENCES

The next thing that will help you discover God's purpose is knowing yourself - your uniqueness, your desires, your gifts, passions, temperament and the positive and negative influences in your life. It is necessary not only to discover the positive but also the negative influences in your life. Discovering these factors and influences will enable you employ God's Word to strengthen the positive factors in your life and bring under control the negative factors.

Not dealing appropriately with these factors will eventually create hindrances that will make it difficult for you to fulfill your God-given purpose. For instance, while the positive influences will work to thrust you forward into God's destiny, the negative influences will at the same time forcefully work to hold you back from God's purpose for you.

Your knowledge of God and yourself will enable you to define and formulate a vision of the life God purposed for you. The vision of God's purpose for your life should be the guiding force in your life. The knowledge and pursuit of your purpose in life will inject you with a surge of energy and strength that nothing else is capable of doing. This spiritual energy will propel you further in the direction towards fulfilling the call and assignment of God on your life.

YOUR LIFE IS A SEED

Listen friend, God placed you on this earth for a specific assignment. Like Moses you were created to deliver people from bondage and lead them to God's designed destiny for them. Like Joshua you were created to lead people from the wilderness of shame and degradation to the Promised Land of hope, peace and prosperity. ***Do not waste your life living unaware of the immense potential and resources God has deposited in you.***

If you have been sleeping, please heed the words of the Apostle Paul in *Ephesians 5:14* which is to *"Wake up Oh sleeper, rise from the dead, and Christ will shine on you."* Paul went on to warn us to *"Be very careful, how (you) live – not as unwise but wise, making the most of every opportunity, because the days are evil."* Please pay attention to his warning that we **"not be foolish but understand the Lord's will (purpose)."**

Did you know, friend that you were born for this time and this hour? Yes, you were born for this hour for a specific purpose and mission. Get to know God in a personal way, get to know who you are, discover your purpose, and start fulfilling it and you will never have one more dull day in your entire life.

You must realize that your life is a seed. Find out the right soil to plant your life and you will grow to become an answer to someone's need. Take an inventory of your life. What do you have to offer someone that can make a difference? What would you attempt to do if you knew it were impossible to fail? Find out! Then attempt it. You will be blessed and also become a blessing to others.

NEVER UNDERMINE YOUR ASSIGNMENT

Never undermine whatever God has called you to do. Remember that a secretary is an answer to the boss's need just as the boss is the answer to the secretary's need. A good wife is an answer to the husband's need just as the right husband is the answer to the wife's needs.

Always think of what God has called you to do as an assignment from Him and a contribution to meet someone's need. Value your assignment and always be thankful for every opportunity you are given to serve God through serving others.

Never look at what you have been assigned to do as just a job. No matter how little or difficult your present job may be, take pride in it and rejoice while you are doing it. God who sees in secret will reward and promote you openly.

CHAPTER TWELVE

LIVING WITH GOD'S PURPOSE: *DEVELOP A HIGH AND BALANCED SELF-ESTEEM*

I praise you because I am fearfully and wonderfully made; your works are wonderful I know that fully well (Ps. 139: 14).

Do not think of yourself more highly than you ought but rather think of yourself with soberly judgment in accordance with the measure of faith God has given you (Rom. 12: 3).

FULFILLING YOUR PURPOSE GENERATES EXCITEMENT AND FULFILLMENT

Purpose! It is the very reason for which you were created. It is the only legitimate reason for living. As a Christian, God's purpose should be the most powerful propelling force in your life. The word of God tells us that our Lord and Savior Jesus Christ was born for a specific purpose - that of destroying the works of the devil *(I John 3:8)*. Do you know your specific purpose in life? If not, you need to find out what it is.

Until you discover your true purpose in life, you will most likely spend your life abusing yourself and others. I am sure that this is not how you want to spend the rest of your life. So get to work to discover your purpose in life! Pursue and fulfill it and your life will be full of joy and excitement.

A HIGH AND BALANCED SELF-ESTEEM

You will never effectively fulfill your purpose in life unless you develop a high and balanced self-esteem. Self-esteem is the value you place on yourself. It is the value you place on the person you see when you look inside yourself. Self-esteem is the value you assign to the person you see when you look in the mirror. If you like what you see when you look in the mirror, you will assign high value to that person. Consequently, you will do everything within your power to build up, nourish and support him or her. If you don't like the person you see, you will do all you can (consciously or subconsciously) to destroy him or her.

This explains why many people engage in such self-destructive habits as having a promiscuous lifestyle, smoking, drinking, drug abuse, under- and over-eating, pornography, gambling, and so forth. At any time a person discovers his true worth he will do everything within his power to stop engaging in these destructive habits. Until then he will make up all sorts of excuses to justify participating in them.

Your self-esteem is, by and large, the product of the information you accumulate about yourself over a period of time. The source of such information generally determines the nature of its product. The mistake many people make is that of going to the wrong sources for this vital information. Whatever you do, be sure that the information you have about you is from the right source.

Many people go to their friends, families, neighbors, secular scientists, etc. to get information about themselves. They will do this before they go to God who created them. Others resort to secular media and other sources for this important information before they consult with God's operation manual - the Bible. No wonder so many people end up confused about who they are and what they are here for.

Please don't misunderstand me because I believe that some of these sources, to some extent, can be useful for reference purposes. Yet if you are serious about knowing who you are, then you must remember that the God who created you knows you better than anyone else (including yourself). Go to Him through His word and He will supply all the information you need about you *(Jam. 1: 5-8)*.

OPINIONS ARE JUST THAT

Never build your life only on what people say or think about you - whether they are good or bad (Matt. 5: 11-12). It is dangerous to build your self-esteem by others' evaluation of you. This is because some people will say some good things about you that are not necessarily true and others will say some bad things about you that are not true either. That is why you must always bear in mind that people's opinions are just that: opinions.

Have you ever considered the fact that most people are too busy with themselves and their problems to devote enough time to get to know you? If this is the case, then it is obvious that no one else knows you as much as God and perhaps you do. So stop spending all your life worrying about what people think or say about you. Rather, devote some time to finding out what God thinks and says about you.

As important as people's opinions are, (and we should not totally disregard them) they are not nearly as important as God's opinion of you and your opinion of yourself. So strive to maintain a balanced view of yourself based on God's Holy word *(Rom. 12:3)*. Never become too high-minded that you begin thinking that you are above any criticism. On the other hand, never undermine or underestimate your God-given abilities and potential *(Rom 12: 3)*.

Believe in God, believe in yourself and believe in the gifts and potential that God has placed in you. Realize that no one will ever be able to maximize his or her potential or do the impossible without believing in God, himself or herself and the gifts and abilities placed in him or her.

HIGH ACHEIVERS AND HIGH SELF-ESTEEM

Your self-esteem very much determines your level of performance in every area of your life. People with high self-esteem usually perform above average. Those with low self-esteem typically perform below their God-given abilities. This is because those with high self-esteem set high and long-term goals. They generally push themselves further than those with low self-esteem. Those with high self-esteem are typically risk-takers and stand strong under the heat and pressure of life. They can better handle criticism and correction. On the whole, those with high self-esteem are more often than not high achievers.

On the contrary, people with low self-esteem are usually low achievers. This is because they are frequently unfocused and easily frustrated. They lack discipline and have poor organizational skills. They often find it difficult to start and finish a project. They are often discontent and extremely sensitive to criticism. Those with low self-esteem usually feel victimized. As a result they mostly will either consciously or sub-consciously look for reasons for failure instead of mechanisms for success.

Furthermore, those with low self-esteem are frequently emotionally fragile, critical and envious of those they perceive as a threat. Consequently, these people are conditioned for failure. Since your level of performance, for the most part, determines your ability to fulfill your purpose in life, it becomes essential that you develop a high and balanced self-esteem.

YOUR PAST IS OVER (PHIL. 3: 13-14)

If you desire to fulfill God's purpose for your life, then you must put the label of your questionable past behind you. Just as you must not glory in your past mistakes, at the same time you should never let them hold you back from your future.

Think of the well-known bible characters such as Abraham, Isaac, Jacob, David, Peter and Paul the Apostle. Did they make any mistakes at some points in their lives? Yes, they all did! Did God use them in spite of their pasts? Yes! He did. In the same way, God will use you in spite of your past blunders, if you will only allow Him to do so. Your past blunders, limited education, experience, or expertise should not be a reason for not fulfilling God's purpose. If you lack any of these essential tools, then pray that God may help you to acquire it and He will.

Don't stop seeking until you find what you desire. Keep on knocking and the right door will eventually open to you *(Matt.7: 7-8)*. Do not let things such as loss of loved ones during your childhood, out-of-wedlock children, divorce, alcoholic or abusive parents, old age, youth, financial setbacks, or any other similar factor stop you from going on to fulfill God's purpose for your life.

If there is anything you can change so that you can enhance your position in life, by all means do so immediately. If there is nothing you can do, then leave behind that baggage and move on with your life. Don't waste the rest of your life crying over spilled milk because it's already gone.

Many great contributors to life started right where you are now but refused to give up. Indeed, some even started in worse conditions than you are in now. Yet they went on to succeed in life. If they could do it, then you obviously don't have a reason not to try. What if you fail? Then welcome to the family. We all missed it at some point but refused to quit. This is precisely why we are able to encourage you today.

Abraham Lincoln had a long history of failing to win an election to public office. Nevertheless, he refused to surrender to fate or cynics. When he finally won an election, he went on to become one of the greatest presidents that the United States has ever produced.

Booker T. Washington was born a slave. At the time it

was illegal for slaves to read. Washington, however, went on and learned how to read. He read everything he could lay hands on. As a result Washington ended up becoming an advisor to United States presidents. What about you? Are you going to allow your background to stop you before you even start? Are you going to quit before you experience that important breakthrough that you need? Please don't. God wants to do some great and awesome things in and through you. Why not give it a chance?

Let me encourage you to learn from our Lord and Savior Jesus Christ. Naturally He had a reason to quit before He even started, although He refused to quit. He was born with what many today would consider a stigma or a questionable background.

According to the Scriptures, He was conceived of the Holy Spirit before His mother was married, although no one but God and Mary knew the whole truth concerning that situation. Yet our Lord went on to become the greatest man ever to be born. Who knows! Maybe people tried to bring up the question of His background from time to time. Yet at no time do we hear Jesus discussing this. He was too busy fulfilling His purpose to waste any time discussing his past. So stop focusing on your limitations and rehearsing sad stories of your past life! Your past is now history. Move on to your future.

MOVE PAST YOUR WOUNDS

Move past the wounds and scars of yesterday. Find out what the gifts are that God gave you to deliver to the world and look for ways to deliver God's package. Be determined that you will not exit this world before you deliver the last package that your Father sent you to deliver. You were created to be an answer to someone's need. Find out who these people are and deliver to them the answer they need. Don't deny these people.

Right now there are people seeking to discover you so that their needs can be met. There are now people dying and some suffering physically, emotionally or spiritually, waiting for you to show up. They are praying that God will send you as the Good Samaritan to help them out of their desperate conditions. Some people are right now waiting for you to arrive as Moses to deliver them from bondage and degradation. Find out who these people are and with God's help meet their needs. As a result, your life will be especially fulfilled. It's never too late to start. Begin right now!

Just as it is true that someone needs you, it is equally true that some people don't need you. You are not the solution to everyone's needs. It is therefore important for you to recognize those that God sent you to help so that you don't waste His precious time trying to solve problems He never equipped you to solve. Find out what your calling is and stick to it. If you try to help someone and he rejects the help, don't become offended. He might not have been meant to receive your help. God may have someone else who may help him or her. At the same time there is someone else set to receive your help.

Some people have allowed their lives to be so crowded with things outside their call that they literally don't have any time left to pursue their specific call. They wonder why they always feel so tired and burned out. I have discovered that, many times, it is not the assignment that burns people out, but everything else that they add to the assignment.

LET YOUR WORK SPEAK FOR YOU

Have you ever heard the expression that actions speak louder than words? I presume you have. There is no situation to which this truth applies better than the fulfillment of your purpose. How often we waste God's time trying to answer critics instead of doing what He assigned us!

What we fail to realize is that destructive critics are just that and nothing more. Coming up with suggestions that will help you and what you are trying to do is not the objective of some of your critics. Their destructive comments are often aimed at bringing you and whatever you are doing down to their level. These people usually aim at reaching close enough to where they can destroy you and what you are doing for God.

The only answer you can give to such critics is the same one that Nehemiah gave to his enemies, who wanted to stop him from finishing God's assignment. When his opponents tried to distract his attention from his assignment Nehemiah told them, *"I am carrying on a great project and cannot come down (to your level). Why should the work stop while I leave and (come) down to you?" (Neh. 6: 3 NIV)*

A former boss of mine once said to me, "George, always utilize your critics for your benefit." What he meant was that I should listen to my critics and use their comments, if possible, to improve myself. On the other hand, he was advising me to ignore them if their comments could not help me become a better person.

Listen, friend, don't spend all your time defending yourself to your critics or to anyone else for that matter. Even though constructive critics may turn out to be your best friends, don't even allow them run your life. Put most of your energy into what God has called you to do. Use constructive criticism only to improve yourself and the quality of your service to mankind. Listen carefully to your critics, and take time to pray about what they say. If they make any suggestions that can help you improve your position, then use them. On the other hand, if you pray about a suggestion and strongly believe that it will hurt your cause, then leave it alone. Keep on doing what God has assigned you. *Let your work speak for you and let God be your defense*.

Let me re-emphasize the importance of paying attention

to constructive criticism since it can save your life and your God-given assignment. However, don't waste too much of your time responding to those who are pointing only to your weaknesses and don't appreciate your potential.

CHAPTER THIRTEEN

LIVING WITH GOD'S PURPOSE: TIME IS GOD'S MOST VALUABLE GIFT TO YOU

THERE IS A TIME FOR EVERYTHING – ECCL. 3: 1-3 NLT

BORN FOR THIS MOMENT

Do you ever wonder why you were not born two hundred years ago? Have you ever stopped to ask yourself why you were born in or immigrated to your present country of residence? Could there be a reason why you are alive today when you could have died with your other friends? Are you a product of chance and evolution? Or did God create and place you on this earth for a specific purpose?

These are questions that should be very important to you. May I submit to you that you are not here by chance. You are not a product of evolution. You are not on this earth just to make a living; you are here on a mission. God created you for a purpose and has endowed you with specific gifts and abilities to enable you fulfill His purpose. Let me encourage you to discover what these gifts are, and to use them fulfill your God-given destiny.

TIME IS ONE OF GOD'S GREATEST GIFTS

Every moment of your life is a gift from God. You will be called upon to account for its use. Therefore I encourage you to make the most of each moment you have to live on this earth. In that way you will have no regrets at the end of your life. If you don't make the best use of your time here on earth you will have a lot of regrets at the end of your life.

In a sense the value that you assign to your time clearly reflects the value you assign to yourself. In other words, the more you value yourself, the more you will also value your time. If you value your time you will diligently guard it to prevent it from slipping away. You will do so through effective self-discipline that will enable you to assign the highest priority to the things that are the most important to you. Always remember that *the most urgent things are not necessarily the most important things.*

FIRST THING FIRST

To become an effective individual there are some important things to consider. One of those is that you must never allow things that matter the most to be at the mercy of things that matter the least. I have discovered both in my personal life and my observations that hard work and great human relations, as important as these are, do not always translate into personal success. *True success is always the result of the ability to locate the most important things in life and assign the highest priority to them in the daily schedule.* To be effective and successful, one must become a diligent follower of one's deep values and convictions. This is what discipline is all about.

As a pastor, I have discovered that if I am not careful, I can easily become addicted to what I would term, the 'spirit of urgency.' This is the spirit that causes you to believe that the whole world depends on you to be able to function. The 'spirit of urgency' gives you the false impression that without you the world can do nothing. It causes you to want to meet temporal needs to fill an emotional void.

This spirit makes you spend most of your time reacting to so-called emergency situations instead of carefully following a designed course of action. It prevents you from focusing on the most important matters of your life. It deceives one into thinking that he is getting things accomplished when the truth is that he is just busy. This spirit promotes false self-esteem in those who allow it to take control of them.

The major problem with this attitude is that it makes one feel good now but does not help much at the end. This is because those who spend time pursuing the urgent matters always neglect to pay attention to the most important things. As Stephen R. Covey has pointed out, "Effective people are not problem-minded; they're opportunity-minded. They feed opportunities and starve problems. They think preventively."

In other words, *effective men and women have the habit of putting first things first.* They do things that failures would not even dare to try, let alone do them. They do whatever it takes to succeed, even though they may not necessarily like doing them. Their sense of purpose, direction and value usually overrides the desire for pleasure and ease.

SAY NO TO GOOD THINGS

Today we tend to immortalize those who are in popular demand. People expect us to be in demand. The more in demand a person is, the more status we accord him or her. While there is nothing necessarily wrong with being in demand, we must always watch out for some things. First, be careful not to overextend yourself due to others' demands. Secondly, don't lose your sense of call and purpose because of such demands. Furthermore, be sure not to become sidetracked. The fact that you are helping others can become something you use as an excuse for not fulfilling your God-given assignment. Don't let that happen.

Finally, be sure that whatever assistance you render is meeting the real need of the one you are helping. You don't want to spend God's precious time and resources doing something that provides a band-aid but not a real solution to the situation. For example, don't waste God's valuable time to continue counseling an individual who won't apply the principles to his or her situation.

Experience has taught me that not everyone who comes to my office for advice wants to use it to solve his or her problems. Some people just come to seek a relief instead of a permanent solution. Such people normally get offended if you present them the real solution to their situation instead of merely a band-aid.

We must be able to say no to even some good and worthwhile causes, if we desire to stay focused. This will not always be easy since people expect us, and we always feel obligated, to help people. Some of us find it difficult to say no because we are afraid that people will reject us. Some believe that to be "good Christians" they must always say yes. But one thing we must realize is that there is no one man that God has equipped to solve all the world's problems. Therefore He could not expect us to say 'yes" on every occasion that someone makes a request. It is important that you diligently seek God's guidance before becoming involved in anything that will demand your time.

You must hear from God before taking on any major project, especially if it is going to require taking time off from your area of strength. I believe that that is why the teacher in the Book of Proverbs cautioned that we acknowledge God in all our ways so that He will direct our paths *(Prov.3: 6)*.

One thing I have found out is that those who don't learn to say no eventually end up hating themselves. I have also discovered that if you are not careful you can so overstretch yourself that you end up hating the very people you are trying to please. It is at the point that you are able to gather enough courage to say "no" to some things that you will stop deceiving yourself about what you need.

Finally, it is hard for any one to truly respect you without that ability to sometimes say "no". At first some people may misunderstand or even reject you, but eventually they will come to respect you for taking such a stand.

CONCENTRATE ON YOUR PRIMARY GIFTS

One of the major problems people have is that of allowing their time to be consumed with things outside the area of their primary call. Sometimes, out of the desire to demonstrate that no job is too menial and no task is too difficult, we spend an enormous amount of time doing things we are not good at and will never be good at. I don't believe this is God's will for His children.

God's will is that we concentrate on working our primary gifts and abilities until we perfect them to His glory. God will reward us not because we worked hard, or because we worked a lot. On the contrary, He will do so because we faithfully executed the assignment He gave to us *(Matt.25: 14-30)*.

Some gifts are designed to enable us to fulfill our primary purpose here on earth. Others are secondary gifts designed to support our primary gifts. Unfortunately, many have failed to maximize their potential because they spent so much time working in areas outside their primary call. For example, I know people who could have been excellent Bible teachers but who waste an enormous amount of time trying to develop a music career. At the same time, I have witnessed some trying to develop a teaching ministry when they should have concentrated on developing their music ministry. My point is this: discover what God created you for and pursue it with utmost passion and He will bless you in it and in turn make you a blessing. *(Gen. 12:1-2)*.

In closing, let me remind you, dear reader, that you are an answer and not a problem. When God created you, He wanted you to become the answer to someone's prayer. Get to know God in an intimate way and He will reveal to you your purpose. When you discover your purpose, take time to fulfill it. Always bear in mind that you are not here to make a living. You are here on a mission. Find out what that mission is, and fulfill it.

YOU CAN DO THE IMPOSSIBLE

PART FOUR

IN ITS TIME

CHAPTER FOURTEEN

IN ITS TIME:
TIMING - AN IMPORTANT FACTOR IN DOING THE IMPOSSIBLE

―――◦―――

The least One Shall Become A thousand (clan) And the Small One A Strong Nation. I The Lord Will Hasten It In Its (Appointed) Time. (Is. 60:22)

"I will prepare myself and mayhap my chance will come"- **Abraham Lincoln**

THE IMPORTANCE OF TIMING

A number of years ago I was invited to attend a meeting in Atlanta, Georgia. The meeting was organized for a world-renowned minister of the gospel. It took place in the Georgia Dome. In the meeting I exchanged phone numbers with the minister who was sitting to my right.

A few days after the meeting in Atlanta I had a phone call from my new friend. As we spoke on the phone, he told me that the minister whose meeting we attended was his personal friend. He then went on to tell me how up until the last two years before the meeting in the Dome, he used to invite this same minister on a yearly basis to do five days of meetings in his church in the same city of Atlanta. During those five days, the man could not draw enough attendants to fill his church of about one hundred and fifty seats.

In my mind I was wondering what engendered the change from this man not being able to fill a one hundred and fifty seat church to now filling an auditorium of well over fifty thousand seats to capacity. Perhaps the man was now preaching something different than what he'd preached when he held revivals at my friend's church. That seemed, to me, a plausible explanation. However, that was not the case. As a matter of fact, according to my friend, he was preaching exactly the same messages with the same delivery style as he had in the previous years.

One night as I was watching a television program, the Lord supplied the missing part of the puzzle. It came through the story that another minister told about the renowned preacher. To illustrate his message on the importance of God's timing, the young minister told the story of how for years this preacher labored diligently in a little church in West Virginia without much of a result.

The year before he became nationally renowned he was invited by a minister friend to be one the speakers in a seminar that was held in Oklahoma City in the United States. At the end of the seminar this friend decided to broadcast clips of the different sessions on his local television program.

At the time this program was airing, Paul Crouch, the founder of Trinity Broadcasting Network (TBN), happened to be in town and watched the clip of a session that this man did. He was quite impressed by this man's ministry. As a result he got the information, contacted and offered him a spot on TBN. It was this offer to air his teachings that exposed this man's ministry to the nation and eventually to the world. Through this series of events Rev. T. D. Jakes has become one of the best-known ministers in the world today.

What made the difference in Rev. Jakes' ministry? What was it that turned the whole situation around for the man? Was it luck or fate? I don't believe so. I truly believe that it was nothing else but God's timing and providence that made the difference in Rev. Jakes ministry.

One of the things we must remember as Christians is the

importance of God's timing. It is important to understand that for everything there is a season *(Eccl. 3)*. We need to understand that God's "soon" is most times different from our "soon" *(2 Pet. 3:8)*.

Timing is an especially important determining factor in anything God does for and through us. It can affect the ability of a pastor to successfully get the message across to his people. It greatly influences the ability of a ministry to successfully accomplish God's vision. Timing can affect a spouse's ability to convey a message to the partner. It can greatly determine the success of a new product on the market. Believe it or not, nobody knows the importance of timing better than God. Timing is more important in His program of things than most people often realize.

I am sure you will agree with me that it took God's providence and timing to arrange the seminar for T. D. Jakes in Oklahoma City at that time. It took the same timing and providence of God for Paul Crouch to be in Oklahoma City at the time the scripts were aired. The right message was on the television at the right time to get Paul Crouch's attention.

Timing and providence of God have to do with God arranging everything to take place in its perfect time and place. This is an important biblical principle that transcends logic and human invention. This is the principle that God will employ to deal with you and me throughout our entire walk with Him on this earth.

Let me quickly point out that God's timing and providence does not in any way exclude our responsibility. On the contrary, it works hand in hand with our willingness to co-operate with God. We shall discuss this in detail as we proceed into this study.

THE DIFFERENT BIBLE CHARACTERS

God's word is full of different Bible characters whose life-experiences demonstrate the importance of God's timing. For example, we see in the scripture Jacob, the deceiver, who would later become Jacob the Prince. We see Joseph, the proud errand boy and the young dreamer, who was destined to become a humble, yet magnificent Prime Minister. We see Esther, the slave girl, who would later become the Queen of Persia and David, the shepherd boy, who became the king of Israel. With all these people the question was the same: "When would it actually happen?"

Also in the New Testament, we see Simon (the fragile disciple) destined to become Peter the rock; Saul the persecutor of the Way would later become Paul the greatest advocate of the Way. The big question was also "When?"

Many of you reading about these Bible characters may wonder whether or not these stories are actually true. So why don't we forget about these Bible examples for a moment so that we can examine how this important principle can apply in your life.

You probably do remember the time that you believed that God had given you a promise concerning a particular situation. At some point you wondered whether it was going to take forever for that promise from God to be fulfilled. Yet it finally did. And now you can testify that everything took place in God's perfect timing.

However, right now you are waiting for the fulfillment of another word that an evangelist or your pastor spoke over you a number of years ago. You most likely still remember how the man of God ended the prophecy with, "And it shall come to pass quite soon, says the Lord."

Perhaps at this time you are once more wondering why it has taken so long for that promise or prophecy to be fulfilled. Maybe, since the prophecy was spoken over you, everything has remained the same or some things have even become worse. Well, I would like to encourage you to not give up or throw in the towel just yet. Always remember that in the same manner that God has helped you before He will do it again.

Timing is a significant factor as far as God's dealing with our ministry or personal lives are concerned. I can assure you that if you do not give up on God, He will bring to fulfillment all He has promised you *(Joshua 21:45)*. Do whatever is necessary to remain obedient and faithful to God and God on His part will do what you cannot do for yourself.

IT MAY SURPRISE YOU

For many of us it may come as surprise to know that our assignments, whether in ministry or secular life, do not always begin at the time we receive the call. God often begins a work in us long before we are called. He usually continues the work, long after we received the word *(Rom. 8:29-30)*. He begins to prepare us for His blessing long before the promise and continues His work even after the manifestation of the blessing.

We see this pattern repeatedly in the lives of Bible characters such as those we mentioned. Therefore relax, rest, and trust in the Lord with all of your heart and do not lean on your insight. Acknowledge Him in all your ways and He will direct you to His destiny for your life *(Prov. 3:5-8)*. Do not become frustrated by the apparent delays. Remain faithful to God's call and you will discover that no one will succeed in taking your blessing from you.

Always bear in mind that delay is not denial. Right now it may not seem like God cares about what is happening in your life. I can assure you, though, that He is working behind the scene in your situation. He is working to set up crucial appointments for you. When He is through, you will like the finished product. Your weeping may endure for a night, but your joy will surely come in the morning *(Psalms 30:5)*.

THE SEEMINGLY INSIGNIFICANT DAYS

Take David, "the man after God's heart", for example. God knew from the beginning that David was going to be a king. In *1 Kings 16:1-14*, David was anointed to become the next king of Israel after the Spirit of the Lord had left Saul, the first king. If you follow the story of David you will find that it took another seventeen years before David inherited the throne.

The question is: why did God not give the throne to David the shepherd boy soon after his anointing? Why did David have to go back to the farm to continue working as a shepherd boy? Why was it necessary for the anointed king to first become an armor bearer, a court musician, a warrior, and a captain over the "distressed, discontented, and indebted" *(1 Sam. 22:2)*?

I believe that the answer to the above questions is that in God's providence and timing, every minute and every step counts towards preparation for the blessing He has for us.

Take another example: Joseph, the model dreamer in the Scriptures. At the age of 17, God gave him a dream to become a leader *(Gen. 37:5-8)*. It took thirteen years for that dream to be fulfilled *(Gen. 41:46)*. He had to go through the Pit, Potiphar's house, and the Prison to get to the Palace. In our human estimation this does not seem to make any sense at all, just as it does not make any sense to you that God would allow you, His child, to go through what you are now facing in your present situation.

Nevertheless, I want to submit to you that in God's system of operation, some of the most difficult, seemingly insignificant and most boring days of our lives always turn out to be the most important ones. This is because these days lay the foundation for what we shall be in future. Therefore, do not ever disdain the difficult and so-called days of small things in your life. They may later on turn out to have been some of the most important days of your life.

PREPARATION AND PURIFICATION

From the studies so far it is obvious that timing is very

important to God for two reasons:

First, timing is important to God because He cannot bless or use you until He prepares you. Satan will give you anything if he knows that you have not been adequately prepared for it. He knows that a blessing can become a curse if you have not been prepared for it. He does not mind pushing you out to perform tasks you are not qualified to handle. He knows how easy it is to defeat an inexperienced soldier in the battlefield.

I believe that this was what Winston Churchill, the World War II hero, had in mind when he said, *"To all of us comes that moment in life when we are literally tapped on the shoulder to do a very special thing unique to ourselves and our talents. What a pity if that moment finds us unprepared."*

Napoleon Hill, the bestseller author of THINK AND GROW RICH: A BLACK PERSPECTIVE once said, *"Nature cannot be tricked or cheated. She will give up to you the object of your struggles only after you have paid the price."* According to Louis Pasteur, the great missionary doctor to Africa, *"Life favors the prepared mind."* In the minds of these great leaders, preparation was one of the most important factors in life success. If this was their view of the value of preparation, then those of us who aspire to succeed in life need to pay great attention to what they had to say.

Secondly timing is important to God because He often employs the passage of time to purify our attitudes, motives and expectations. How easy it is to allow God's vision to be fouled up by our personal agendas and ambitions! God uses the waiting period to build into us His character. During this time, He develops in us some characteristics such as love, joy, peace, patience, gentleness, goodness, and self-control. He inculcates within us other qualities like commitment, dedication, faithfulness, contentment, perseverance, and integrity. He uses little responsibilities to prepare us for greater ones.

During these trying times in your life, learn to wait on

God for His anointing and direction. If you can faithfully wait on Him during the difficult times in your life, then it is likely that you will be faithful when you get into the ministry. In the ministry, you will be able to wait on Him faithfully for anointing and direction. Josiah Holland puts it this way, *"There is no achievement that is not the result of patience, working and waiting."* And finally as the Apostle Paul puts it through *"faith and patience"* we will *"inherit that which has been promised" (Heb. 6: 12).*

A number of years ago, I read the autobiography of a young drug addict who was a popular rising rock musician in South Africa. After he was miraculously saved, his pastor told him, *"Here's what we want you to do. We want you to sit in the church for at least three years - no music ministry, no preaching, and no nothing."* The young man's reply was: *"Pastor, you know what is best for my life. God brought me here for a purpose, and I am ready to learn."* It is important to note that the pastor's instruction to this young man was to not minister for three years. He did not tell him not to train and develop his musical talent and skills during this period of time.

Today that young man has become one of the most functional and well-known men in the prophetic ministry. After the period of waiting, the pastor blessed and released the young man to a very successful ministry. Some of you readers have been blessed by the prophetic ministry of Kim Clement, the South African, and did not know how he started. Now you know how far God has brought him from where he started. Praise God who always rewards our obedience in patience *(Heb. 11:6).*

AN AARON TO THREE PASTORS
One of my friends has called me a number of times to seek advice concerning leaving his job to go into full time preaching ministry. Each time he called I sensed in my spirit

that the timing was not right. Consequently, I advised him each time to keep his job, which of course he did. Today he is still working the same secular job. However, over this period of time, God has given him a thriving ministry, which many would like to have. Now we often talk and laugh about those days when he wanted to quit his job even though he did not have the slightest idea what he wanted to do after leaving his job.

Over the last number of years this man has became an Aaron to the last three pastors of his church. Also, through God's providential circumstances he was asked to take over as the teacher of a fledging couples Sunday school class in the church. By the grace of God he built up the class to become the largest and most dynamic in the entire church.

In 2003 my friend was selected as the state of Georgia Sunday School Teacher of the Year and the National Sunday School Teacher of the Year in one of the largest denominations in the United States. At the time he started working on this project he was the chairman of the Board of Trustees of his home church of about seven hundred members.

In 2003 he was also elected the chairman of the search committee for a new pastor to replace his former pastor who resigned to take the position of the state superintendent of his denomination. In these positions my friend has been blessed to become close to the different pastors of the church. As a result he has been blessed with a ministry while training on the job.

It would not surprise me if my friend one day ends up in some form of full time Christian ministry. If this happens, he will go out not only with a wealth of experience but also with a lot of favor. On the other hand, if he doesn't end up in full-time Christian ministry, Enefiok Umana will still be remembered by those of us who know him as a very successful servant not only of God but also of His people.

STUDY TO SHOW YOURSELF APPROVED

Are you now being tested by the word of the Lord as Joseph was *(Ps. 105:16-21)*? Let me encourage you again to make the best use of it and not throw away this time. While you are waiting on the Lord for your breakthrough, use this time to study and meditate on the word *(Ps. 1: 1-3)*.

Spend this time in prayer both for yourself and others in need. Pray that God may enable you to trust Him and to exercise self-control in all matters. Remain faithful in whatever little things He may have you to do and use this time to learn how to faithfully trust Him while waiting on Him for anointing and direction.

While waiting, implore Him to remove impediments from your path and impurities from your heart, your agenda, and motives. If you do this, you will be pleased with the outcome of diligently waiting on Him. You can't actually miss Him waiting on Him this way.

CHAPTER FIFTEEN

IN ITS TIME:
THE TWO CALLS: FIRST TO LOVE AND THEN TO SERVE HIM.

―――――

But when God, who set me apart from birth and called me by His grace, was pleased to reveal His Son in me so that I might preach Him among the Gentiles, I did not consult any man (Gal. 1: 15-16NIV).

TWO CALLS UPON EVERY BELIEVER

One of the most frustrating things for a believer is to know that God has a specific calling upon his life that is different from what he is doing at the moment. Yet one thing we must realize is that for every one of us there are two calls that God has placed upon our lives. The number one call is that of remaining obedient on a day-to-day basis to the revelation He has given us in His word.

For the most part, God is not going to trust us with a specific assignment until we have learned to obey Him on a daily basis in the general revelation given us in His word. This is why we must relax, rest, and concentrate on putting to practice every general principle He has, so far, revealed to us in His word. If we remain faithful in what He is now calling us to do then in His appointed time He will reveal to us His specific assignment.

IT CAN BE VERY DANGEROUS

Many people make the mistake of jumping ahead of

God. They think that just because they feel the compulsion of God's call they should run off and do something. Doing so can be extremely dangerous at times.

One of the dangers of stepping ahead of God is that it can lead to frustration and confusion. One can end up in the dark with no anointing or God's presence to sustain him in the job. Remember that except the Lord builds a house those who do so labor in vain *(Ps. 127:1)*.

The second danger of running ahead of God is that it can delay the fulfillment of God's plan for your life. Take Moses as an example. There is no doubt that God raised him up to be a deliverer for the Israelites. However, he stepped out to fulfill the call before either he or his people were ready for what God was going to do.

Moses was not ready because as we know he resorted to delivering his people with the arm of flesh *(Ex.2: 11-12)*. He should instead have waited for God's time when He could deliver the people through Him *(Ex. 3: 7-8, Ex. 12: 29-32)*.

The Israelites were not ready for Moses' leadership because we see them rejecting it when he first offered it *(Ex.2: 14)*. However, forty years later when Moses and the people were ready, it was easy for the Israelites to accept Moses' leadership *(Ex.4: 27-31)*. God often prepares both the person and the mission before He brings them together in its time.

Finally, jumping ahead of God can lead to a lot of hurt both for the person and others associated with him. How often families have suffered because someone ran off to "serve the Lord in full time service" before he/she, or the family, was ready!

Who knows what pains Moses might have caused his parents by him being forced to run away to Midian! We already know that in the case of Joseph, the father was caused a lot of grief *(Gen. 37:34-35)*. Waiting on the Lord to birth and fulfill His plans and purposes in our lives is not the easiest thing to do, but the rewards are often worth all the waiting *(Is. 40:27-31)*.

AFTER GOD'S SPECIFIC CALL

One of the most dangerous things that can happen to an individual is for him to become successful before he is prepared. In these days of instant food and internet communications many have come to also believe in instant success in every aspect of life.

One of the consequences of the press for instant success is that we see a lot of people playing the roles of copycats. In an attempt to reproduce success some have lost their originality. They forget that each of us is unique and special and God loves us and wants to use us as we are.

An attempt to be someone else in your job or ministry will first lead to confusion because there is no way you can possibly be another person successfully. You are unique and special to God. He has a special place in His overall plan for you that no one else can occupy. By trying to be someone else, you are actually denying Him the right to be God in your life and the opportunity to use you in a unique way *(Ps. 46: 10)*.

If you have discovered what God's specific call on your life is, take time to develop it and grow in it. Find someone who is successful in what you desire to do. Submit yourself to the person and learn the principles of success from him without losing your personality or uniqueness.

Most of the time, the Lord will have you submit yourself for training under a godly person who has the experience and expertise in the area to which God has called you. Sometimes, of course, He may give you an on-the-job training. Find out what God's will for you is and follow it diligently.

UNIQUE AND SPECIAL

It is true that the mantle of anointing can fall from one ministry to another. It is also true that when we start off we may behave like or exhibit some characteristics of people that we admire and under whom we are studying. That does not necessarily mean that God wants to duplicate that person.

Whatever happens, we must remember that God wants us to be unique. That is why He gave you a fingerprint and DNA that will match no one else's. Let God develop you into the unique and special person He desires you to be.

God is no respecter of persons. However, He has a special place in His heart for you. Let your frequent prayer be that His hands will be upon you for good and that He will reveal His Son in you in a unique and special way *(Gal. 1:15)*.

It is always good to spend time reading, studying, watching the video teachings and listening to anointed audiotape messages. Studying other materials by godly men and women is something every believer must be humble enough to do. However, in doing so, we must remember to ask the help of the Holy Spirit. This is because what you receive from others are only facts and information until the Holy Spirit turns it to revelation. It is only the Holy Spirit who can turn information to revelation *(1John 2:20-27)*. Therefore you should always look to God as your source of revelation, even when studying works of other godly men and women. After all, it is the spirit that quickens; the flesh profits nothing *(John 6:63)*.

THE KEY TO SUCCESS

One key to success in what God has called you to do is faithfulness. This includes first of all remaining faithful, diligent and devoted to the general call of God in His word. For example, God has called upon all Christians to obey His word not as a requirement to get to Heaven but as a symbol of our love and respect to Him.

Faithful obedience to God's commands in every day situations is His general will for us as His children. Such include the commands to walk in love, forgive as God in Christ has forgiven us, be patient with one another, be kind to each other and so on. As we fulfill His general will on a daily basis, then we obligate Him to reveal to us His specific will such as what profession we need to specialize in, who we should marry, which home we should buy or which church we should attend.

The reason that God does so is that the person who is faithful in the general call of God will most likely remain equally diligent and devoted to the specific call when he discovers it. If you remain faithful and humble in your general dealings in the affairs of life, God will honor you by revealing to you His specific call on your life. So don't be overly concerned about missing God's specific call if you are now faithful in your obedience to Him in every day matters.

Even if you have missed Him in your present calling, if your heart is right, He will find you. He is the God of hearts. Does He not promise that we shall seek Him and find Him if we seek Him with all of our hearts *(Jer.29:13-14, 2Chro.16: 9)*? In *Rom. 8:28* God promises that all things will work together for the good of those who love God and are called according to His purpose. This promise is for all of us His children.

Now let me ask you my friend: Do you love God and believe that you were called to salvation through His promises? If so, then you can be sure that all things will work together for your good – even the apparent mistakes in your life.

As I close this part of our study, let me encourage you to remain faithful in your present call. Until you discover God's specific call, be patient and remain faithful in your obedience to His general will. Do not run off to engage in anything until God directs you. Consult with mature godly men and women but do not go to them for quick answers on how to become an instant success.

Wait on God until He shows you even when to consult with mature godly people *(Gal.1: 15-17)*. Spend time in fellowship with God after He has revealed to you His specific purpose for your life and He will lead you from one day to the next. Your best job is the one you are working right now. Be faithful in it until God leads you to something else.

I once heard of a man who sold his farm to go to a foreign country to seek a fortune. The only unfortunate thing was that right in that farm was a diamond mine that he was not aware of. The man who bought the farm discovered the diamond deposit and therefore became a multi-millionaire while the former owner was still traveling around the world looking for a fortune.

The lesson of this story is this: Stay where you are right now and develop your farm. The chances are that you may discover a diamond deposit right where you are!

CHAPTER SIXTEEN

IN ITS TIME:
HE WILL NEVER FAIL

⟞⟝

Let each man remain in that condition He was called. Were you called while you were a servant? Don't worry about it, but if you are able to be free, rather, do that. (1 Cor. 7:20-21).

HE WILL NOT LEAVE YOU (HEB. 13: 5)

God has placed two calls upon your life. The number one call is to be a Christian on a day-to-day basis, mirroring the character of Christ as you obey His word. The number two call is to a specific and unique position in the Kingdom of God. Until you discover God's specific mission for you, be content in your present state and wait for God to place you in the specific call at the right time.

Are you just getting out of a bad relationship? Please don't rush into another relationship until God heals you of the hurts of the last relationship. If you do, you may end up more miserable and hurt since you are most likely going to be attracted to another hurting and wounded person. When two hurting and wounded people enter a relationship, the result is always more hurts and wounds.

Have you just lost a job? Please don't rush to accept anything that comes. Pray and wait on the Lord to lead you to the next place of employment. Don't accept anything unless you are in total peace about it *(Phil. 4: 6-8).* Are you single at the moment? Please don't rush out to get someone just because you feel lonely. Enjoy this time that God has given to you while waiting on Him to bring you the right partner.

Your present position may seem totally unrelated to God's call for your life. Yet if you trust Him, you will find out that all things will work together for your good because you love God and are called according to His purpose *(Rom.8: 28)*. If you trust Him, He will provide for you even from unexpected sources until He leads you to the next step *(Is. 40: 27-31)*. If you have ever trusted God, this is the time to do so with all of your heart and do not lean on your understanding. In all your ways acknowledging Him, knowing that He will direct your path *(Prov.3: 5-8)*. According to God' word those who wait on Him will ultimately mount up with wings as eagles, run and not be weary, walk and not faint *(Is.40: 27-31)*.

THE TIME TO SEEK THE LORD (Hos. 10: 12)

Just because the brook has dried up on you does not mean that God has left or forsaken you. The end comes for the believer when the Lord appears and that is not bad news at all. Therefore use this time to wait on the Lord until He reveals to you His specific purpose for your life. Don't be in any hurry to become engaged in anything. Stop running to people for quick solutions for your situation. Patiently wait on God for His solution instead.

When God reveals His plan to you, you must approach it with both faith and caution. Never operate in fear because God has not given us the spirit of fear but that of power, love and self-control. On the other hand, don't operate in presumption or foolishness either, because He has given us the spirit of sound mind (wisdom and self control) *(1 Tim. 2:7)*. When you discover your specific call, spend enough time to develop and mature spiritually before you step into it.

THE FIRM FOUNDATION (Ps. 75: 6)

In *Galatians 1-2* Paul shares some principles, to which

every believer should pay particular attention. In these portions the apostle Paul pointed out that when he first received the call to go to the Gentiles he had two options to choose from for His preparation. One option was to go to the other apostles to learn quick and easy ways to become a successful apostle. There would have been nothing wrong with that. The other option was to go to the Arabian Desert where he could wait on the Lord to reveal Himself to him *(Gal. 1: 15-17)*.

Paul chose to go to Arabia and spend time alone with God. Three years later he returned to Jerusalem to become acquainted with Peter and stayed with him for only fifteen days.

In his approach to his call Paul exhibited the wisdom that is lacking today in many who are called to the ministry of the word. After his call he withdrew to spend sometime alone with God so he could hear and learn from Him. Then he went back to fellowship with the brethren; perhaps to compare what God told him with what the other brethren had learnt from the Lord while they were with Him.

Three principles are to be noted in this account of Paul. The number one principle is that neither publication nor isolation is the answer to growth and development of your call. The number two principle is the need to spend time alone with the Lord, Himself, seeking His wisdom after He has revealed your specific calling to you. And finally, it always helps to confirm with other mature Christians the new revelation you believe you have received from the Lord.

There will be times that it will be necessary to withdraw from the crowd so you can spend time alone with the Lord. Nonetheless, after such season of prayer and study, you must return to fellowship and share with the brethren what you learnt during your quiet time with Him.

How often do people try to use all kinds of gimmicks to promote their ministries and gifts! The only problem with this is that if you need these types of methods to promote your ministry, you will also need them to sustain it. The promotion achieved from these kinds of methods is usually shaky and temporal.

Nonetheless, when God promotes you, the promotion will sit on a firm foundation *(Ps.75: 6-7)*. So let God promote you and publicize your ministry for you. Your part is to remain faithful to the present task and concentrate on developing your personal relationship with Him. Your ministry is never going to be stronger than your personal relationship with God.

The seemingly slow progress in their vocations easily frustrates many people. As a result, they are often willing to take short cuts to speed up the process. You want to be careful, not to try to circumvent God's process to attain progress. If you do, you will pay a high price for your impatience. Never try to force your promotion. Instead take time to lay a good foundation and the promotion will come at its proper time.

Finally, be open to learn from any person who is walking close to the Lord, provided he is willing to help. Seek out and learn from people of proven record of success in the area you believe God is calling you to. As Dr. Leroy Thompson, Sr. always says, "Be always ready to submit to leadership and not to control."

But does this necessarily mean that we should not use modern technology and means to promote the gospel? Absolutely not! Does it mean that we should not use the modern means and technology to promote our ministry? I don't believe so. The truth is that if you are going to present the gospel effectively to the contemporary world, then you must be sure to bring yourself up to date with current events and technology. You must also be willing to employ these latest means available to market your product.

However, you must be willing to wait on the Lord to

show you when, and to open the right doors for you to gain access to the available means. Remember that God's timing is crucial in anything that we do. Employ the most effective means to present the gospel and trust in God to give you the maximum result from your effort.

Don't try to use the gospel to manipulate on anyone. God is big enough to persuade and draw people that are ready. He knows when to open the right doors and at the same time He will close the wrong ones *(John 10: 2-5)*. Until He opens the door, leave it closed and when He does open the door don't hesitate to walk through it.

EVERY MOVE BY GOD'S REVELATION

While it is important to pray for increase and expansion in your ministry or vocation, it is even more important that people know of what God is doing in your life and thank Him for you. What God is doing in you is as important as what you are doing for Him. If God has done nothing in you, what you do for Him may not have much of eternal value.

I once heard Joyce Meyer say that while she was praying for her ministry to grow, the Lord told her that there was no need for a tree to bear much fruit unless the roots were firm and deep enough to sustain it. I personally would rather have a strongly rooted tree with few fruits than a tree with so many fruits and not enough strong roots to sustain them. It will be just a matter of time before the latter is brought down by the weight of its fruits.

It may be a long time from your last move to the next, but it will be worth the waiting. The late Dr. Kenneth E. Hagin once told his spiritual sons and daughters that he would rather be too slow than too fast. It feels good when you know that you have made a move that is going to lead to progress in your life. However, always be sure to ask the Lord for grace, wisdom and guidance before you make any moves. Be sure not to compromise God's call or vision in an attempt to make some progress. You will ultimately lose anything you compromise your deeply held convictions to obtain.

FOCUS ON THE ONE WHO CALLED

Oppositions to God's call always emerge somewhere along the way. Do not be deterred by such oppositions. The devil's tactic is to get your eyes off the Lord so that he can throw you off God's course. Keep your eyes on the One who started the work in you and He will finish it *(Heb. 12: 1-3)*.

Co-operate with other people whenever possible, even with those whose views may differ from yours. However, take a strong stand for convictions and the call that God has placed upon you. Show the greatest respect to everyone that God puts in your path but don't be distracted by what is going on in other people's lives.

Never try to bring people to your side or win approval by either changing or compromising God's vision. If you do, you will eventually lose whatever you got by being disobedient to God's vision.

If you compromise your vision to earn respect, you can be sure that you will lose that respect somewhere along the line. On the other hand, if you take a strong stand for your deep convictions, even your opponents will later respect you for them. So keep your head high and trust in the Lord and He will see you through the toughest times in your pursuit of God's destiny upon your life.

YOU CAN DO THE IMPOSSIBLE

PART FIVE

WALKING IN DIVINE FAVOR

CHAPTER SEVENTEEN

WALKING IN DIVINE FAVOR: *THE NEGLECTED SPIRITUAL TOOL*

―――◦―――

Now when the turn came for Esther...she requested nothing but what Hegai the king's eunuch, the custodian of the women, advised. And Esther obtained favor in the sight of all who saw her (Esther 2:15).

But by the grace (favor) of God I am what I am, and his grace to me was not without effect. No, I worked harder than all of them–yet not I, but the grace of God that was with me (1 Cor. 15: 10).

THE NEGLECTED SPIRITUAL TOOL

As believers in Christ, the spiritual forces of faith, love, joy, hope, patience and perseverance must control us. It is extremely difficult to function effectively as Christians without the operation of these spiritual forces in our lives. In many Christian circles there is the recognition of the importance and necessity of these spiritual tools in our lives.

However, there is an important spiritual tool to which most average believers have not been exposed. Consequently, these believers have not been able to tap into its benefits. That neglected spiritual tool is ***the force of divine favor.***

The force of divine favor is one that every believer who desires to engage in the faith-walk must be aware of and understand. As a matter of fact, we cannot truly operate in faith without the propelling force of God's favor. In this study we will examine this vital spiritual force.

A DYNAMIC AND PROPELLING FORCE

The spiritual force of divine favor is one of the most dynamic and propelling forces in the Christian's faith-walk. ***God's favor will thrust you into victory during an intense fight with the devil.*** It will empower you to become a blessing, thus enabling other people to avoid misfortune in their lives. The favor of God will thrust you into extraordinary experiences, which will release God's influence to work for you and through you on the behalf of others. ***God's favor will influence situations, people, and places for you.*** It will open doors for you that no one can close and close doors that no one can open.

When you walk in God's favor, He releases to you extraordinary spiritual, material and financial support. God's favor will release to you supernatural support in everything you do. It will make the rough places smooth and cause streams to spring forth for you in the desert *(Is. 43:18-20)*. God's favor will make things easier for you where other people find it hard to do the same things.

When you begin to operate in God's favor, it will bring you needed provision in times of desperate need. It will open ministry doors for you, give you advantages in situations. Divine favor will grant you special privileges just as it was with the patriarchs, Abraham, Isaac, Jacob, Joseph, David, Daniel, Nehemiah and Ezra.

Things around you will begin to change once you recognize, confess and begin to operate in the spiritual force of God's favor. If your desire is to walk by faith then you must be ready to operate at all times in expectation of divine favor.

WHAT IS IT?

So what is this divine favor that we are talking about? What is this dynamic spiritual force that can accomplish so much for God's people?

The American Heritage Dictionary defines favor as: 1)

A gracious, kind, or friendly attitude, 2) An act evidencing such an attitude, 3) A friendly regard shown by a group or a superior 4) Approval or support; sanction, 5) Advantage and 6) To make easier or more possible.

From the above definitions we can conclude that God's favor has to do with His kindness that places us in an advantageous position beyond what could be or what is naturally expected. It carries with it an emblem or mark of approval that puts the recipient in a special position of advantage. In a sense we can say that God's favor is synonymous to God's presence, His grace, preference, His Hand and His provision.

Throughout the scriptures, we find that extraordinary things took place because God's people operated in God's favor. Such people included Joseph, Daniel, Ruth, Esther and a number of others that we have previously named.

IF IT WERE NOT FOR HIS GRACE

Enobong and I truly believe that if it were not for God's special favor upon us we would not have been able to do what we are now doing in our ministry. There is no natural explanation to what has happened in our lives and ministry over the past thirty years.

There is not one person who has observed our ministry over the last twenty years who would not admit that there is something other than human abilities that have propelled us to where we now are in the ministry. We believe that the supposedly unknown factor in the equation of our life is the favor of God.

Like Paul the Apostle, Enobong and I can declare to God's glory, "But by the grace of God I am what I am. And His grace to me was not without effect." Thank God for His divine favor, for what could we have done without it?

When we speak of God's favor we are referring to God being with you, working with you to influence people and situations for your advantage. When you walk in God's favor, He influences people to make decisions that will benefit you, sometimes without even being aware of it.

WALK BY FAITH AND EXPECT GOD'S FAVOR

It is true that as believers in Christ we must walk by faith and not by sight. Nonetheless, just laboring in faith alone will not always get the job done because there are times that your faith may be weak or not sufficient to carry you through the situation. Just because faith is exhausted does not mean that we have to play dead or accept defeat. When our faith is weak we can trust God's favor to carry us over. Faith will not and cannot override favor. They work hand in hand with each other. When God's favor overshadows you, your work is cut up for you. When you take off in divine favor, life's gravity will lose all its hold on you.

Your faith in God and in His word is a vital part of your walk with God. Keep in mind, though, that there are some things that God alone must do for you. There are some things that God can get to you without too much of your effort or faith. He will get them to you because He is God your Father. There is a certain push or thrust that comes with God's assignment and if you let God He will turn it on your behalf. When that thrust gets into operation, no power on earth will be able to hold you back.

YOUR DAILY CONFESSION AND EXPECTATION

As Christians, we must <u>constantly</u> be aware of and remind ourselves of God's favor towards us. We must constantly confess and expect to operate in it. ***We must constantly confess that we are surrounded by God's favor.*** Confess regularly that you operate in God's favor.

Confess that God releases His influence to work for you in your business, ministry and personal transactions. He did it for Joseph in Egypt even though he was a slave *(Gen. 39:2-6)*. God is no respecter of persons. Just as He did it for

Joseph, *(Gen. 39:21-22)* He will certainly do it for you.

God's favor caused Daniel to excel even in the land of captivity *(Dan. 1:9)*. He received favor with the Babylonian authorities because God was with him. *(Dan. 1:9)*. The same favor of God caused the king to promote Daniel to a position of honor and authority *(Dan. 6:24-28)*. That same spiritual force is waiting to operate on your behalf if you will let it.

Let me encourage you, friend, to purpose in your heart from this day that because you are His child you will walk in God's favor. Decide that by His grace you are going to be on top and not beneath, the head and not the tail *(Deut. 28:13)*. Decide from this day forward that good things will always come your way because of God's favor. And if any bad things come your way, God's favor will turn them around for your good because you love Him and are called according to His purpose *(Rom. 8:28)*. ***Refuse to go around with a victim's mentality. Decide from today that you are victorious even in the present trying situations you are facing.***

IT IS NOT ALL UP TO GOD

Let me emphasize, my friend, that it is not all up to God whether you are blessed or not. Yes, it is God who releases the blessing. Or put it another way, God has already blessed you. ***However, you and I must prepare the right atmosphere for God's blessings to be revealed in us.*** See yourself as blessed and you will be eternally blessed. See yourself as cursed or denied and your vision will be fulfilled *(Num. 13:33)*.

Believe it or not we all carry a mental blueprint or image of ourselves. Sometimes it is not distinctly defined to the casual observer. Nonetheless it's always there. The individual who sees himself as a failure will find some way to fail, irrespective of his good intentions and the opportunities that may be available to him.

The person who views himself as a victim of circumstances and environment will eventually find something in his environment to support his viewpoint. Our behaviors, actions and feelings will always verify our self-image. This will be the case in spite of our conscious efforts to come out with a different result.

So you see friend that it is not all up to God, your environment, friends or even your enemies for that matter, what the final outcome of your life will be. You have a lot to do with it. Whether you realize it or not, friend your strongest enemy is never the giant in your Promise land but the grasshopper in your head. Get rid of the grasshopper in your head and you will be able to subdue the biggest giant in your land.

It is, therefore, time for you and me to wake up and aggressively go for that which is ours in Christ. *(Eph. 5:14: 17)* Refuse to be denied and to blame other people for not having what you need in life, your family and for your ministry. Go into God's Word and find out what belongs to you. Believe in those promises that God has given to you in His Word. Now go ahead and confess those things like they are already yours because they *are* yours. *(John 15:7) We walk by faith and not by sight.*

God says you are His favorite. Don't be shy! Go ahead and believe it. And if you believe it, confess it in the face of any adversity. Confess that you are the favored of the Lord. Don't wait for your circumstances to change before you confess it. Confess it and refuse to do otherwise until your circumstances change. Your circumstances have no alternative but to yield to God's Word *(Mark 11:22-24)*.

SEE YOURSELF AS GOD SEES YOU

Nothing that people do to try to thwart God's favor in your life will succeed if you walk righteously before Him. Laban tried to stop Jacob by changing his wages several times but he did not succeed because Jacob was favored of God *(Gen. 31:7-9)*. Haman tried to eliminate the Jews from the face of the earth, but he failed because they were favored of God *(Est. 7)*. Potiphar's wife tried to stop Joseph but he stood for what he believed and finally ended up ruling Potiphar's wife *(Gen. 39:21-23, 41:44-45)*.

The enemy sought to destroy Esther and David but failed because they were walking in God's favor. Jealous opponents tried to set Daniel up to destroy his life and ministry but they failed. Daniel spent a night in the den with lions and came out the following day unscathed because he was favored of God *(Dan. 6:1-28)*. I can tell you that no weapon formed against you will succeed because you walk in God's favor *(Is. 54:17)*.

NOT OVER YET; JUST ANOTHER BEGINNING

Right now the enemy wants you to think that the fight is over and that you have lost. ***But you can look the enemy in the face and proclaim your victory in spite of what you see in the*** *natural (1 Sam. 17: 34-47)*.

Always take note of these facts as you go through life: God's favor will produce recognition for you as it did for David, even if you are the least likely to receive it (1 Sam. 16:22). God's favor will produce pre-eminent and preferential treatment for you as it did for Esther *(Est. 2:17)*.

God's favor will cause your petitions to be granted even by ungodly civil authorities as it was with Esther *(Est. 5:8)*. His favor will cause rules, regulations and laws to be changed and reversed to your advantage as it was with her *(Est. 5:1-2)* and Daniel *(Dan. 6:21-28)*. God's favor will produce increase and supernatural promotion for you as in the case of Joseph. It will restore *everything* that the enemy stole or kept back from you as it did with the Israelites in Egypt *(Ex. 3:19-21)*.

Divine favor will produce honor for you in the midst of your enemies *(Ex. 11:3)*. It will increase your assets, especially in real estate. *(Deut. 33:23)* **It will give you victory in**

the midst of great impossibilities. *(Jos. 11:20)* Now do you believe what I just told you? If so, then begin to confess and shout about them. God bless you!

In the next chapter I will be sharing with you the message on ***Divine Favor*** that the Lord gave me at the end of 2004 to share with our partners and friends.

CHAPTER EIGHTEEN

WALKING IN DIVINE FAVOR: *YOUR YEAR OF DIVINE FAVOR*

But by the <u>grace of God</u> I am what I am, and His grace to me was not without effect. No, I worked harder than all of them—yet not I, but the grace of God that was with me (1 Cor. 15:10 NIV).

For promotion and power come from nowhere on earth, but only from God. He promotes one and deposes another (Ps.75: 6-7 TLB).

At the end of the year 2004 I asked the Lord to give me a word that will set the course for both our partners and church members in the year 2005. In answer to my request, He said to me, "Go tell my people that this will be for them the year of the overflow of my favor." He said, "Tell my people to be prepared for the year of an unprecedented outpouring of my favor to them." As a result of the instruction I started teaching on the topic, **"Walking in Divine Favor."**

Some testimonies confirming God's word have already started coming in at the time of writing this chapter. One lady shared a testimony of how God extended His favor to her the next day after sitting through one of the teachings in our church. She had a job interview a day after sitting in one of the teaching sessions. In that particular session I mentioned that God's favor would cause people to be so impressed with you that they would move someone to create a position for you. After her interview this lady was told that the company did not have an open position that would fit her qualification at the time. However, she was told that they were so impressed with her that they would move someone up in position so that they could hire her. This is just one of several testimonies that have come as a result of the teaching. I pray that as you read this article, God will enable you to receive and apply the principles expounded in this message to your personal situations. Better yet, call our office and order the series on *"Walking in Divine Favor"*. The tape series contains a lot more information than we have in this chapter.

Some of you may be asking, "So what is this divine favor that you are talking about?" You see friend, God wants to help you not only in the monumental situations in life but also in the little matters concerning you. He wants to accomplish this purpose by extending His divine favor to you.

The word *favor* in the Bible is the same word translated *grace* in some portions of the Scripture. It is that gracious, kind or friendly attitude extended to an individual. Favor usually carries with it the sanction, support and the approval of a superior that makes things easier and more possible in certain situations.

Divine favor has to do with God's support and enabling to get the job done. It is the anointing that causes you to prosper in your assignment. It removes burdens and destroys yokes so that you can have the environment conducive to fulfilling God's purpose for your life.

Divine favor will put you in an advantageous position so that you can do the job that God has assigned to you. It will provide an added aid and advantage to enable you to fulfill your call. It provides the assistance to get the job done. It is sometimes referred to in the Scriptures as "the grace of God", "the presence of God" or "the Hand of the Lord".

Divine favor will cause people to give you preferential treatment and to go out of their way to help and support you. Some of these people will help you without even understanding why and in spite of the fact that they may not even like you.

When you operate in divine favor as Abram, Joseph and Ruth did, God's blessings chase and overtake you. Doors open for you that will be closed to other people and you receive preferential treatment, even from those who don't particularly like you. God will bless the works of your hands and that of all the people who are close and supportive of your call, when you flow in divine favor. Everywhere you go, things will turn to your favor and people will go out of their way to help and support you. So I encourage you to take this truth seriously: receive it with humility and then watch God perform His word in your life.

AN ACCELERATION OF THE PROCESS

What are other benefits of understanding and applying this truth in your personal life? First, as you receive and appropriate the truth of this message to your situations, you will experience an acceleration of the process of blessings in your life.

As you step into the anointing to walk in divine favor, you will experience more sudden and immediate breakthroughs than ever before. For instance you will experience the acceleration in the answers to your prayers.

As it was with God's people in the past, you will henceforth start to experience an overflow in the harvest of the seeds you have sown over the years *(Amos 9:4)*. For receiving and embracing this truth, the harvest for your seeds will multiply and come in faster this year than the seeds you plant. You will experience more harvest for your seeds this year than at any other time during your walk with God.

Because of the divine favor in operation in your life, you will experience sudden miraculous reversals of past misfortunes in your life *(2 Kings 7: 1-2, 7:17-20)*. More than ever before, you will experience this year more sudden reversal of misfortunes in your life than at any time in your entire life. As in the case with the prophetic students, who lost the borrowed iron axe head *(2 Kings 6:1-7)*, many miraculous recoveries of lost possessions will take place in your life starting this year.

Those who owed you or robbed you of anything will be forced to return to you what they took from you. You will experience huge supernatural debt reduction and cancellation as it was with the prophet's widow *(2 Kings 4: 1-7)*.

The favor anointing will miraculously and dramatically wipe away your financial debts. Some things you thought were lost forever to the enemy will be miraculously recovered this year. For example, your lost spouse and other relatives will suddenly return to the Lord. Your children that ran away from home will this year return as the prodigal son did. Your spouse that abandoned you and your children that turned against you will seek reconciliation with you this year.

Many of you will experience supernatural promotions to positions of prominence and influence as it was with Esther *(Esther 2:16-18)*. Those of you reading and appropriately applying this truth will experience huge profits in your businesses and promotions at your individual workplaces.

Miraculous protections from the enemy's attempt to destroy you or yours will occur this year as you operate in divine favor *(Dan. 6:19-22)*. When the enemy shall come against you, like a flood the Spirit of the Lord will lift up a standard against him *(Is. 59: 19)*. No weapon formed against you this year will prosper and every tongue that rises against you in judgment court will be found to be at fault *(Is. 54:17TLB)*.

PREREQUISITES TO CONSTANT DIVINE FAVOR

There are some prerequisites to experiencing constant manifestation of divine favor. One is to **develop confidence** *in God's favor* – the belief that God loves you enough to always extend His favor to you.

Another prerequisite to walking in constant divine favor is to **expect God's favor to operate on your behalf in every situation** – good, bad, big or small. Also **constant flow in God's favor requires consistent obedience to God's word.** You cannot consistently live like the devil's child and expect God's continued favor to be extended to you.

Having said that, let me give you a word of caution: Be always careful that your expectation is from God and not from men *(Ps.62: 5, 65:5)*. For example, don't go around telling your sad stories to people, seeking sympathy. If you have any requests let them first be made to God. Of course, this doesn't mean that you should not ask for prayers or even help to meet your needs when necessary. However, don't go around flashing your bills expecting people to pay them for you. As a Christian, you must avoid taking unnecessary advantage of people's goodness and generosity. When your faith is in God He will show you what to do in every situation and will move in people to extend favor to you. Yet don't go around flashing your bills expecting people to pay them for you.

You must develop faith and confidence in the fact that God's favor will kick in to help you in every adverse situation you may face from this point on. This means that you must believe that God will step in to heal, deliver you and restore back to you whatever the enemy stole from you.

Even more, believe that He will bless you in normal circumstances and conditions when you are not facing any trials. Remember that God is not there only when you are in trouble. He is there for you all the time.

God loves you just as He does Jesus and will do for you whatever He would do for Jesus. God will cause you to receive preferential treatment when you need it. He will open closed doors for you and close doors that need not open. He will set a table before you even in the presence of your enemies and anoint your head with oil. He will fill your cup to overflowing and cause goodness and mercy to follow you all the days of your life, if you will just believe. The key is to develop confidence in His favor and expect it all the time.

EXPECT GOD'S FAVOR EVERY DAY IN EVERY SITUATION

Learn to speak God's favor over every area of your life. Speak God's favor over your marriage, finances, job situation, and physical health. Declare God's favor over your children, employees or bosses. Expect God's favor to bring you out of your adversity and turn everything around for you just as he did for Joseph, Ruth and David. When you are going through difficult times, like Paul and Daniel, expect God's favor to kick in to deliver you. Don't throw a pity party when you are facing trying and hard times; instead thank God for the opportunity for Him to show out on your behalf.

I am confident and I expect to be treated differently. I believe that people will always want to help me and be a blessing to me. These are not arrogant statements but statements of fact. You too must start to believe, declare and expect God's favor to operate in your life. Every day before you leave the house, be sure to thank God for His favor that will open doors and make the day an easy one for you. You don't have to pray loud or make a big deal out of it. You can declare it under your breath and believe that it will happen as you have declared. Your life and death are in the power of your tongue.

In your darkest hours stay in the attitude of faith and declare the favor of God and nothing will be able to bring you down. Satan would like to see you throw in the towel and quit, thinking it's over. Don't listen to his lies. Your Dad controls the time and if you need extra time for a comeback He will give it to you.

It's only over when God says it's over and He will not stop the game before you win. So don't be discouraged in your trials; instead expect the favor of God to work for you. Always remember that though your weeping may endure for a night your joy will certainly come in the morning.

We Would Like To Hear From You

The primary purpose of writing this book is to equip you, the reader, with the information that, hopefully, will help you to maximize your potential. God has deposited in everyone such wealth that can help the person do the naturally impossible things. Most people die without tapping into this reservoir of God's wealth in them.

Our prayer is that the information we have just shared will help you begin to seriously consider rising up to become everything that God created you to be. If this book has been of help to you, we would like for you to do three very simple things for us:

1. Recommend it as good reading material to someone else.
2. Contact and share your thoughts with us.
3. Take a few minutes to pray that God may enable us put it in the hands of everyone who can be blessed by it.

To contact us write to:

N. George and Enobong Utuk
The Word of Faith Ministries, Inc.
P.O.Box 4676,
Eatonton, Georgia 31061

About The Author

Dr N. George Utuk, born and educated in private Christian schools in Nigeria, earned a diploma in Theological Studies from South Wales Bible College in South Wales (U.K.) in 1976, a Bachelor of Arts (B.A.) in Religion and Philosophy from Southwestern College in Winfield, Kansas (U.S.A) in 1978, a Master of Arts (M.A.) in Political Science from Wichita State University in Wichita, Kansas (U.S.A.) in 1981 and a Doctor of Philosophy (Ph.D.) in Political Science from Atlanta University (currently known as Clark Atlanta University) in Atlanta, Georgia (U.S.A.).

Dr Utuk is a prolific teacher of the Word who combines his exegetical knowledge of the Word with a great sense of humor. He has been in ministry and has been teaching the Word since 1971. He and his wife have been in full-time ministry in the United States since 1990.

Dr. Utuk's ministry experience also includes an extensive travel in Nigeria and the United Kingdom in the seventies to teach and preach the word. He has been the president of the African Christian Fellowship, Atlanta Chapter and the vice-principal of Southwest Atlanta Christian Academy, a private Christian school in Atlanta, Georgia.

Dr. Utuk's ministry has also enabled him to travel

extensively to different parts of the United States. In addition, he has traveled to the countries of Brazil, Israel, Jamaica and Nigeria for missions.

Dr. Utuk is currently the founder and president of the Word of Faith Ministries, Inc., a non-profit religious organization registered in Georgia, U.S A. He is also the pastor of the Abundant Life Word Fellowship in Eatonton, Georgia, U.S.A. His conversion testimony has been published in "Today's Challenge" and he is the author of numerous articles published in The Word of Faith ministries' monthly newsletter "The Living Word".

Dr. Utuk has been married for twenty- nine years and lives in the United States with his wife Enobong and his daughter Ibiangake.

References

1. Caldwell, Kirbyjon H. with Mark Seal. The Gospel of Good Success: A Road Map to Spiritual, Emotional, and Financial Wholeness. Simon and Schuster: New York, NY 1999.
2. Copeland, Kenneth and Gloria. From Faith to Faith: A Daily Guide to Victory. Kenneth Copeland Publications: Fort Worth, Texas 1992.
3. Copeland, Gloria - How to Walk on the Water (video teaching) Kenneth Copeland Publications: Ft. Worth, Texas.
4. Covey, Steven R. The Seven Habits of Highly Effective People. Fire Side Books: Simon and Schuster, New York, NY 1989.
5. Graham, Stedman. You Can Make It Happen: A Nine-Step Plan for Success. Fire Side Books, Simon and Schuster: New York, NY.
6. Hilliard, I.V. Mental Toughness for Success: Proven Biblical Principles for Successful Living. Light Publications: Houston, TX, 2003.
7. Jakes, T.D. Maximize the Moment: God's Action Plan for Your Life. G. P. Putnam's Sons: New York, NY.

8. Kimbro, Dennis and Napoleon Hill. Think and Grow Rich: A Black Choice. Baltimore Books: New York, 1992.
9. Macaulay, Ray. Making Your World Different. Rhema Publishing: South Africa.
10. Ortberg, John. If You Want to Walk on the Water You've Got to Get Out of the Boat. Zondervan Publishing House: Grand Rapids, MI 2001.
11. Roberts, Oral. Still Doing the Impossible. Destiny Books, 2002.
12. Winston, Bill. Divine Favor: A Gift of God. Bill Winston Ministries: Oak Park, IL, 2002.

Printed in the United States
40229LVS00003B/166-1509